WELCOME ON BOARD

WELCOME ON BOARD

A BEGINNER'S GUIDE TO SAILING

RAMON GLIEWE

Translated and adapted by
BARBARA WEBB

FREDERICK MULLER LIMITED
LONDON

This edition first published in Great Britain 1981
by Frederick Muller Limited, London, NW2 6LE
First published in West Germany in 1978 by Verlag Delius Klasing

British Library Cataloguing in Publication Data

Gliewe, Ramon
Welcome on board.
  1. Sailing
  I. Title   II. Webb, Barbara
  797.1'24   GV811

  ISBN 0-584-10384-0

Typeset by Computacomp (UK) Ltd
Fort William, Scotland
Printed in Great Britain by Butler & Tanner Ltd
Frome and London

List of Contents

Introduction

It may be when you stand by the water's edge on a sunny summer's day that you are first tempted into learning how to sail. You see a cheerful, sun-tanned couple arrive, step on board one of the boats, bustle about and, soon, there is a rattling noise as the sail is raised. One of the crew unties the boat and shoves off gently; the sail flaps about in the breeze until the other crew member pulls on a rope attached to it. As he pulls a rod at the back end towards him the boat turns, leans over slightly when the wind fills the sail, and slips away silently. Can sailing really be as easy as that?

Then comes the day when you find yourself sitting in a sailing boat for the first time. Everybody on board is busy preparing for a sail, and you hear the crew using expressions that you never knew existed, as well as familiar words with strange new nautical meanings, such as 'painter', which here is the rope that ties the dinghy to the shore, and 'sheets' which here control the sails. You may feel useless and stupid and probably decide despondently after a quarter of an hour at most that you will never be able to learn how to sail − let alone understand the jargon. But other crew members were once complete novices too, and if they could learn, then so can you.

Nautical language stems from the days when, almost without exception, seamen were male. Today the helmsman or crew could equally be a woman, and it is common to find a boat crewed entirely by females. Traditionally a boat is 'she', and it is generally easier to understand the text if her crew (whether male or female, or both) are referred to as masculine.

The boat herself

A boat is the brain-child of a naval architect or designer, whether she is one of many identical series-produced boats or an expensive custom-built one-off. The designer provides the builder with a set of line drawings from which the boat is constructed. The three plans that show the shape of the hull, which is the body of the boat, are the profile or sheer plan, the half-breadth plan and the body plan. They show respectively the side view, the bird's eye view and the view from one end. The designer also draws the sail plan and, for larger boats, provides an accommodation plan which shows how the cabin and all the below decks area are to be laid out.

A good 90 % of the sailing boats under 46 ft (14 m) in length that are exhibited at the major international boat shows are made of glassfibre reinforced plastics (GRP) a synthetic material which has virtually replaced wood, the traditional material for boat-building. Some lightweight sailing dinghies are made of plywood, and a few boats are built of steel, but this last material is so heavy that it is only an attractive proposition for boats over about 26 ft (8 m) in length. Still fewer boats are built of aluminium which, although ideal for boat-building, is so expensive that it is used almost exclusively for high performance racing keelboats when cost is unimportant. The very small number of ferro-cement boats are mainly amateur-built, and are of considerable size because the material, cement reinforced with metal rods and wire, is relatively very heavy.

Centreboard boats, Keelboats, Bilge-keelers and Multihulls

Boats vary so greatly in design, size, character and cost that every sailor can find the right boat to match his temperament. A boat may be designed for racing or for cruising, and to be sailed single-handed or with a large crew on board. The waters in which she will sail may be inland, close by the coast or offshore. She may be a motor-sailer, designed to perform as well under engine as under sail, an extremely expensive, luxuriously appointed cruiser, a highly-sophisticated racing machine, or a very cheap and simple dinghy, amateur-built from a kit.

Most sailing boats fall within the two categories, keelboats and centreboard boats. A keelboat has a fixed ballast keel which extends downwards beneath the hull. This discourages her from making leeway, that is from being blown sideways through the water by the wind, and also increases her stability by counteracting the pressure

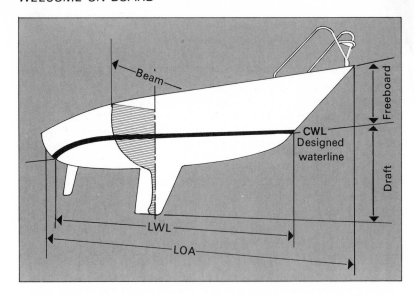

of the wind which forces her to heel (to lean over to one side). A boat is said to be tender if she reacts to the wind by heeling quickly, whereas a stiff boat does not heel so easily.

Centreboard boats such as sailing dinghies do not have a ballast keel; instead they have either a pivoting centreboard which protrudes through a slot in the bottom of the hull, or a daggerboard which is raised and lowered vertically. The centreboard is lowered to reduce leeway when sailing towards the wind or with the wind abeam (blowing from one side), but is raised when sailing downwind, or to run up onto a beach. Whereas a keelboat depends largely on the weight of her ballast keel for stability an unballasted centreboard dinghy depends on the shape of her relatively beamy hull. The crew also help to prevent her from heeling by shifting their weight to windward.

A centreboard dinghy is not seaworthy; she can be blown over – capsized – relatively easily and is suitable only for sailing inland, in estuaries and close by the shore. She must not only be unsinkable but able to float while supporting all her crew, even when swamped and full of water after capsizing. Most dinghies have air-filled buoyancy bags or built-in watertight buoyancy compartments which may be foam-filled. Some have double bottoms, others have hulls with a foam core sandwiched between solid inner and outer plastics skins. Centreboard dinghies are not self-righting; they have to be turned right way up by the crew after they have capsized.

2

FIGURE 1: PARTS OF A BOAT

Forward means at, near or towards the front end of the boat, the bow, as opposed to aft which relates to the back end, the stern. Amidships is either midway between bow and stern, or midway between the sides. The centreline or fore-and-aft line is the straight line amidships between bow and stern; athwartships is at right angles to the centreline. Length overall, LOA, is the boat's length along the centreline between the foremost point of her bow and the aftermost point of her stern. The hull, the body of a boat, is partly immersed in water, and the topsides are the part of her sides that are above the water. They are separated by the waterline from the bottom, the part of the hull beneath the water. The term wetted surface or area includes the bottom, rudder and keel or centreboard. The maximum speed of a boat depends on her waterline length, (LWL), and this is measured along the fore-and-aft line between the points where the waterline cuts her stern aft and her stem forward. The forward and aft overhangs which extend beyond the waterline provide reserve buoyancy. The bilge is the area where the hull changes from being mainly horizontal underwater to being mainly vertical above the water.

Beam is breadth measured at the widest point, and the shaded area shows the shape of half her midship section at this point. The topsides of a boat that has tumblehome curve inwards at the top, maximum beam being somewhere between the waterline and deck level, whereas flared topsides curve outwards from the waterline and beam is greatest at the sheer line. Freeboard is measured from the waterline to the gunwale or deck at the top of the topsides. A boat with normal sheer has higher freeboard forward and aft than amidships, but most smaller modern keelboats have slight reverse sheer, freeboard being higher amidships than at bow and stern. Draft is measured from the waterline to the lowest point of the keel and differs from the draft calculated by the designer because the load on board varies, just as the waterline at which a boat floats varies with load from her designed waterline. A boat is said to draw the number of feet or metres of water that corresponds to her draft, and she will be aground, not afloat, if the water is less deep than that figure.

The rudder aft is either turned to the left to make the bows turn to the left, to port, or to the right to make her alter course to starboard.

A keelboat can sink because the weight of her ballast will pull her down if she fills with water, say after springing a leak or after being holed in a collision. On the other hand she is self-righting because her heavy ballast keel will turn her to float upright, on an even keel, after being knocked down by a strong gust of wind – heeling at an angle of 90° with mast and sail lying flat on the water. She will even right herself from an upside down position if she turns turtle in a storm.

Some boats are a compromise between these two basic types. Shoal-draft centreboarders with a centreboard as well as a shallow ballast keel are generally self-righting and can sail in shoal waters when the centreboard is raised. They are much more stable than a centreboard dinghy on account of the weight of the ballast keel, and are easier to transport on land than a keelboat. A boat with a retractable keel is even easier to load onto a trailer because the whole keel can be raised into the hull, sometimes leaving just the bulb of ballast beneath the bottom. She too is self-righting and suitable for sailing in shoal waters.

Bilge-keelers are particularly suitable for sailing in tidal waters. When the tide ebbs the water level falls and the boat settles comfortably on the bottom to dry out standing upright on the long shallow twin keels which are bolted to the hull along the bilge either side. Performance under sail is generally inferior to that of a traditional design with a central ballast keel.

Then there are the multihulls. A catamaran, often abbreviated to cat, has two identical hulls, while a trimaran has a central hull with an outrigger or float either side. The relatively rare proa has one hull and a single outrigger; most proas sail with the outrigger always on

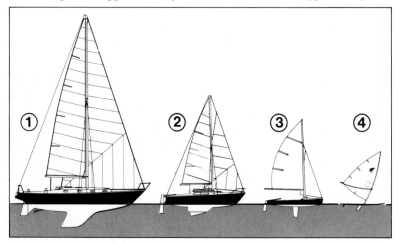

FIGURE 2: BOAT TYPES

1. Fin and skeg keelboat: this boat has a short deep fin keel, and the rudder is hung beneath the hull on a skeg near the stern.
2. Keelboat with centreboard: the centreboard is lowered to discourage the boat from making leeway when she is sailing towards the wind or with the wind abeam. When she is sailing downwind the centreboard is raised and housed in a slot in the relatively shallow ballast keel. Wetted area is reduced and this enables her to sail faster than a comparable keelboat when reaching and running. Here the rudder is hung on the transom.
3. Sailing dinghy: the bottom is almost flat and there is a centreboard or daggerboard instead of a ballast keel.
4. Sailboard: a flat buoyant board with a small daggerboard and a tiny fin aft. The boardsailor stands on it, supporting the sail and the mast, which is connected to the board by a universal joint.

4

the downwind side of the hull, to leeward. Transverse members connect the hull(s) and outriggers of multihulls, some of which are ballasted, while others are not. At small angles of heel these fast boats are extremely stable on account of their exceptionally great beam but they capsize when they heel beyond a certain angle, just as dinghies do. They are much more difficult to right than monohulls, especially if they turn turtle, because they are just as stable when floating mast downwards. Buoyancy is often provided to ensure that the mast will not sink – usually in the form of a float at the top of the mast. The accommodation of cruising catamarans and trimarans is generous by comparison with that of keelboats of the same length, but they take up a lot of space when moored or anchored. Open racing catamarans are fast and exciting to sail, and the Tornado has been selected as an Olympic class.

Although sailboards race under the same racing rules as normal sailing boats they can hardly be classed as boats. A sailboard has no rudder to steer with, and no hull – just a flat buoyant board like a long surfboard on which the boardsailor stands, supporting the mast

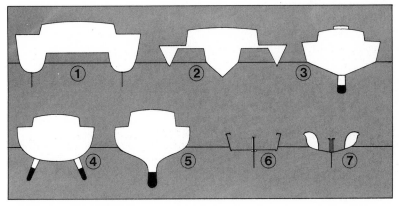

FIGURE 3: HULL SHAPES

1. Round bilge cruising catamaran. The cabin spans the gap between the two hulls.
2. Hard chine cruising trimaran. The cabin is concentrated amidships over the central hull, and the outriggers either side serve as floats. In larger trimarans the outriggers may provide additional accommodation.
3. Hard chine boat with a cabin: the ballast keel is bolted to the hull. Typical of a steel hull.
4. Round bilge hull with shallow bilge keels: good for cruising in tidal waters because the boat settles upright on the bottom when the tide ebbs and water level falls.
5. Typical round bilge cruiser with ballast keel.
6. Hard chine flat-bottomed sailing dinghy.
7. Modern round bilge dinghy with built-in buoyancy tanks either side.

and sail with his hands. He steers by tilting (raking) the mast further forward or aft and, instead of using sheets to control the angle of the sail to the wind, he pulls the wishbone boom itself in and out manually.

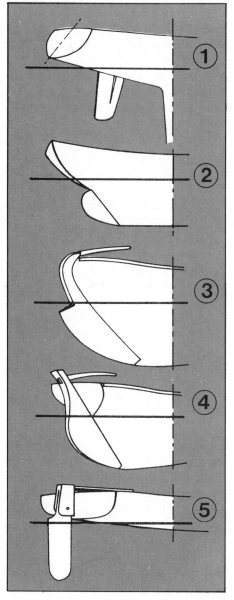

FIGURE 4: STERNS

1. Counter: the short overhang and counter raked forward are typical of many modern designs. The free-standing spade rudder projecting beneath the hull is a balanced rudder, part of the blade area being forward of the stock about which it pivots.

2. Canoe stern: bow and stern are much the same shape, with the topsides converging to a point. The rudder is hung on the after end of the keel.

3. Norwegian stern: a pointed stern which is relatively rare although it has proved to be very seaworthy. The rudder is easier to repair than that of a boat with a canoe stern.

4. Transom: the rudder, hung on the transom of this traditional keelboat, can be unshipped easily when necessary.

5. A racing dinghy's transom: the broad flat run aft encourages her to plane.

The midship section of most boats is either rounded or angular, that is, either round bilge or hard chine (Fig 3). A chine is where two flattish areas of planking or plating meet at an angle, and if the boat has more than one chine either side she is said to be double chine or multichine. Hard chine boats are carvel-built with smooth topsides, as are most round bilge boats, but some wooden boats are clinker-built with each plank overlapping the plank beneath like roof tiles.

A beamy boat with a full midship section is stiff and has high initial stability; when she is floating upright she initially resists the tendency to heel in response to the wind, whereas a narrow boat with low initial stability heels quickly, even when the wind is light.

The way a boat behaves under sail depends to a considerable degree on the shape of her underwater body viewed from the side, her lateral plane. The bottom, keel or centreboard and rudder resist sideways movement and discourage her from making leeway. The directional stability of a boat with a long keel that extends fore-and-aft along much of her length is good; she tends to sail steadily on course but is slow to react when the rudder is turned to one side, and sails relatively slowly because frictional resistance is high. A boat with a short keel and a separate rudder near the stern answers the helm readily when the tiller is put over to deflect the rudder, but is more difficult to keep on a straight course. She sails faster because frictional resistance is lower.

Weight also affects boat speed. Fast racing dinghies are very light and sail area is relatively large. The term displacement is used for keelboats; a heavy displacement cruising boat with a long keel displaces a greater volume of water and sails more slowly than a comparable light displacement offshore racing boat that has a short keel and is constructed of lightweight materials.

The rig

A sailing boat is also categorised by her rig, namely by the number of her masts and sails, the shape of the sails, and how they are set. In earlier centuries sailing ships were square-rigged and set square sails, but virtually all sailing boats now are fore-and-aft rigged. Apart from the few boats that are gaff-rigged or carry spritsails and lugsails, boats are bermudan-rigged and set the triangular bermudan sails that were introduced in Europe some 50 years ago.

A boat has at least one mast. The mainsail is hoisted with its luff attached to the mast, or to the mainmast if the boat has more than one mast, and is spread by a spar (a pole). The foot (Fig 5) of a

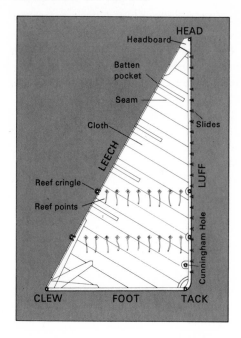

FIGURE 5: THE PARTS OF A SAIL

The upper edge of a quadrilateral sail is the head: the top corner near the mast is the throat, the top outer corner the peak. Here the leech runs straight from head to clew but most sails have a roach which extends beyond the direct line. Two reefs can be tucked in. The camber or fullness of the sail can be adjusted with the Cunningham Hole which is pulled down to flatten the sail in fresh winds.

bermudan sail is spread by the boom and the head of a quadrilateral sail by a gaff, sprit or yard. A headsail such as a jib or genoa is set forward of the foremost mast in the fore-triangle; this is the area between the mast, the deck and the forestay which supports the mast from forward. A staysail is usually set on a stay.

Una rig (Fig 7) is the simplest of all, and is the normal rig for one-man centreboard dinghies. The mast is stepped well forward and only one sail is set.

A sloop (Fig 7) has a single mast, usually stepped slightly forward of amidships, a mainsail and one headsail. The number of sloop-rigged keelboats and centreboard dinghies far exceeds the total number of boats with other rigs.

A cutter (Fig 7) also has one mast but carries two headsails, the jib being set forward of the staysail. Cutters are particularly popular for cruising because two small sails are easier to handle than one large one, and sail area can easily be reduced when the wind freshens by lowering one of the headsails.

Yawls and ketches (Fig 7) have two masts, the mainmast forward being taller than the mizzenmast aft. Although the number of sails set can be varied to suit the wind strength, and extra sails can be hoisted to increase sail area in light breezes, sloop rig is aerodynamically more efficient. When compared with the mainsail, the mizzen set on the mizzenmast of a ketch is larger than that of a yawl. Because sail area is divided more evenly between the two masts ketch rig is often preferred for larger ocean-going cruising boats which may be sailed short-handed, that is, with a smaller crew than normal.

The schooner (Fig 7) also has two masts, but the mainmast aft is as tall as or taller than the foremast. Schooners perform less well than boats with other rigs on almost all points of sailing, but some sailors support their qualities enthusiastically.

Working sails are the basic sails set by a boat in moderate to fresh winds, namely the mainsail and jib of a sloop, plus the staysail of a

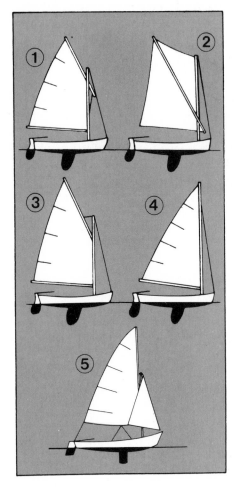

FIGURE 6: TYPES OF SAIL

1. Lugsail: the head is extended by the yard, the foot by the boom.
2. Spritsail: the sprit runs diagonally from the tack to the peak. The Optimist, designed for young children, sets a spritsail.
3. Gaff sail: the head is bent to the gaff which has jaws that fit closely round the mast.
4. Bermudan sail: the triangular sail which has replaced almost all other sails, such as gaff sails and spritsails.
5. Gunter rig: the yard is hoisted to form an extension of the mast, both often being short enough to stow inside the hull of a dinghy being trailed. The four-sided sail appears to be triangular because the angle between the head and the luff is almost 180°.

9

cutter, or the mizzen of a ketch or yawl. In light to moderate winds the jib is often replaced by a genoa; this may well be larger than the mainsail which it overlaps. When running or reaching, many two-man racing dinghies and most keelboats set a large sail called a

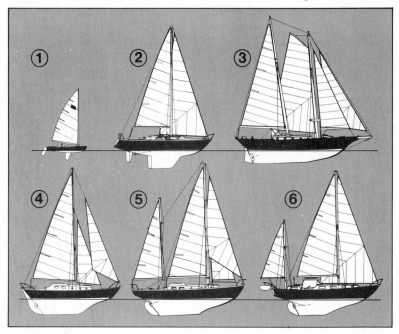

FIGURE 7: RIGS

1. Una rig: one sail set on a mast stepped well forward. The sail may be loose-footed, that is, connected to the boom only at tack and clew.

2. Sloop: one mast, a mainsail and only one headsail. This boat is masthead-rigged; her foretriangle extends to the top of the mast whereas that of a fractional-rigged sloop, such as the Star in Fig 56 only reaches about three-quarters of the way up the mast. With her short deep keel and separate rudder aft this boat's lateral area is concentrated amidships.

3. Schooner: the foremast, stepped nearer the bow, is the same height as, or shorter than the mainmast. Although here the foresail set on the foremast is a gaff sail this schooner is bermudan-rigged because she carries a bermudan mainsail.

4. Cutter: one mast and two headsails, the jib being set forward of the staysail. The long keel and transom-hung rudder are typical of a traditional heavy displacement bermudan cutter.

5. Ketch: the shorter mizzenmast aft is stepped forward of the rudder stock.

6. Yawl: she too sets a mizzen on her mizzenmast which is stepped abaft the rudder stock but, when comparing the area of mizzen and mainsail and the height of mizzenmast and mainmast, the yawl's mizzen is relatively smaller and her mizzenmast much shorter than those of a ketch.

spinnaker, while yawls and ketches may also set a mizzen staysail or a mizzen spinnaker. Offshore racing boats sometimes set an additional sail called a tallboy to improve the rig's aerodynamic efficiency, or a big boy to increase sail area further when sailing with a fair wind. In heavy weather small storm sails, which may be made of heavier canvas, replace the working sails, the trysail being set instead of the mainsail, and a spitfire or storm jib in the foretriangle.

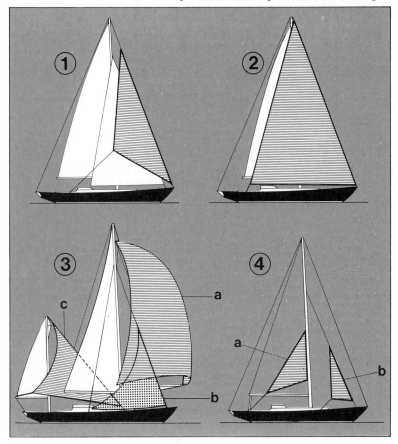

FIGURE 8: ADDITIONAL SAILS

1. Cutter with a large yankee jib and staysail for light airs.
2. Sloop or cutter with a very large, light-weather genoa, the area of which is considerably greater than the area of the mainsail which it overlaps.
3. Sails set by a yawl or ketch when reaching or running downwind: (a) spinnaker, (b) spinnaker staysail, (c) mizzen staysail.
4. Storm sails: (a) the trysail, set in place of the mainsail; normally is not sheeted to the boom, (b) spitfire or storm jib.

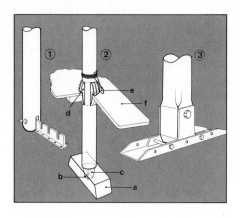

FIGURE 9: STEPPING THE MAST

Masts are either stepped on the keel or on deck.

1. This dinghy mast, stepped on a toothed rack, can be shifted forward or aft to tune the rig and improve balance.

2. Keel-stepped mast: (a) keel, (b) step, (c) foot, (d) wedges, (e) waterproof mast coat to prevent leaks, (f) deck.

3. Lowering mast stepped in a tabernacle mounted on deck on a fore-and-aft track. The mast pivots about the bolt through the tabernacle cheeks.

FIGURE 10: STANDING RIGGING

Masthead-rigged boats with a forestay leading to the top of the mast do not require jumpers. The boat in the centre has diamonds (a) which are extended either side of the mast by the upper spreaders (b). The upper shrouds (c) are extended by the lower spreaders (d). (e) lower shrouds.

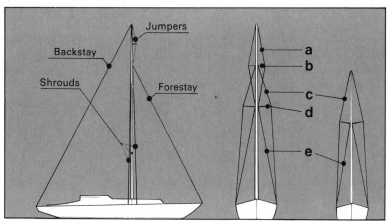

Standing and running rigging

The term rigging embraces all the wires, ropes, pulley blocks, fittings and gear that support the mast and control the sails. Standing rigging, which provides permanent support, consists of shrouds that lead from high on the mast to the sides of the boat to brace the mast laterally, and stays that provide fore-and-aft support, the forestay from forward and the backstay from aft.

The larger the boat the taller the mast and the more complicated will the standing rigging be. A few dinghies such as the Finn, (Fig 57) have entirely unsupported unstayed masts, but most simple centreboard dinghies have a forestay and one pair of shrouds. The masts of larger dinghies and smaller keelboats are usually supported by a forestay, a backstay and two pairs of shrouds, the upper pair being held away from the mast by spreaders (Fig 10). Larger keelboats have jumper stays and struts or diamonds, more than one pair of spreaders and extra pairs of shrouds to support the topmast. Boats with fractional rig, such as the Star in Fig 56 have running backstays, or runners, instead of or as well as permanent backstays. Runners lead from the point where the forestay is attached to the mast to the side decks either side about half way between mast and stern. They are classed as part of the standing rigging although they are manned when sailing, the leeward runner being slacked off to allow the sail to set properly and the windward runner being set up taut with a lever. The upper ends of shrouds and stays are attached to tangs on the mast, and the lower ends are connected to rigging screws which are shackled to chain plates bolted to the hull; the rigging screws are turned to adjust the tension of the rigging. Lighter alternatives for dinghies are shroud and stay adjusters, or simply a lanyard (light line).

Running rigging consists of all the wires, ropes, blocks and gear that move and control part of the rig, such as a sail or a spar. Halyards, which hoist sails, run over a block or sheave at or near the masthead and down to the deck. Sheets trim sails by adjusting their position relative to the fore-and-aft line to suit the wind direction. Headsail sheets are shackled to the clew and lead back either side of the mast and into the cockpit. With a small mainsail, the mainsheet is usually rove through a block on the boom and another which slides athwartships on a track or horse fitted either on the afterdeck or centrally in the cockpit, however the mainsheet of a larger sail is rove through several blocks to reduce the effort required from the crew. Downhauls and topping lifts control the vertical position of spars, and guys control their horizontal position. A hoist raises the centreboard and the outhaul pulls the foot of the mainsail out along the boom. The kicking strap prevents the boom from lifting.

Chandlery, gear and fittings

Before the boat can be taken out for a sail she has to be fitted out with all the equipment which enables the crew to control her. Many of the items needed in addition to sails, spars and rigging are illustrated in Figs 11, 12, 13, 14, and 15. Those that link one part to another include hanks and slides that hold sails to stays and spars, and shackles that connect ropes to part of the gear. Other fittings control the direction in which a rope leads; the sheave (roller) at the masthead, for example, converts a downward pull on the main halyard into an upward pull that hoists the mainsail. Usually the jib halyard is rove through a block attached to the mast near the top of the forestay. Jib sheets are led through a fairlead or block on the side deck, and spinnaker sheets are rove through a turning block right aft and then lead forward into the cockpit. Halyards and sheets are often belayed to cleats, but dinghy sheets are either held in the hand or cleated in quick-release jam cleats. The anchor cable is made fast to a sampson post, bitts, or mooring cleat bolted to the foredeck. Many controls and fittings may be used to enable the crew to alter the shape of the sails to suit the direction and strength of the wind, the most common being a sliding jib fairlead (Figs 11 11, 13 19, 14 24).

FIGURE 11: CHANDLERY AND FITTINGS

1. Light alloy single block.
2. Similar double block; the two sheaves turn on a single pin.
3. Tufnol single block with swivel.
4. Fiddle block: two sheaves on separate pins, one above the other. Often used for a dinghy's mainsheet.
5. Swivelling foot block with a cam jam cleat, suitable for a dinghy's mainsheet.
6. Ratchet block.
7. Mainsheet track with a traveller that runs on rollers.
8. Double boom claw or reefing claw. The claw encircles boom and sail and is wide enough for several layers of sail to be rolled round the boom when reefing.
9. Slide: this one slides in a track on the mast or spar, others slide over the track.
10. Piston hank: attaches jib, genoa or staysail to a stay.
11. Jib sheet track with adjustable fairlead.
12. Fairlead for a dinghy's jib sheet.
13. Track fastened to the forward side of the mast so that the spinnaker pole, which fits into the bell, can be raised or lowered as required.
14. Spinnaker pole end fitting with piston closure.
15. Cam cleat with fairlead: grips a sheet or other rope.
16. The clam cleat also grips rope: often used for centreboard and lifting rudder hoists, or mainsheet traveller controls.
An assortment of shackles used to connect a wire or rope to a sail, fitting etc.:
17. Swivelling shackle.
18. Piston snap shackle.
19 and 20. D shackles: the former is stainless steel strip, the latter galvanised iron or gunmetal.
21. Twisted shackle.

Whenever manual power is insufficient, extra power can be provided mechanically by a winch or, as in the case of the sailing dinghy's centre mainsheet in Fig 13, by rigging a tackle consisting of a rope rove through several blocks.

Some items are not illustrated, such as the boathook which is a pole with a hook at one end, used to pick up an object from the water or to push something away from the boat (fend off) or vice versa. The rudder of a dinghy has a finger-like pintle which is dropped into an eye called the gudgeon, and there is often a retaining clip to prevent the rudder from being unshipped and lost accidentally. Some sailing dinghies have oars and rowlocks so that they can be rowed home when the wind drops, but most have a

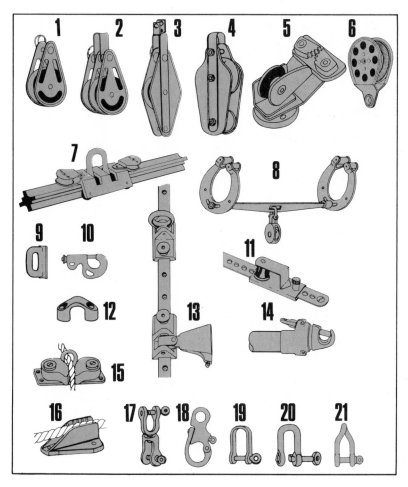

paddle. Water shipped on board has to be removed, and this is scooped out of a dinghy with a bailer or pumped out of a keelboat's bilges (the lowest part of the hull where water collects) with a bilge pump. Most larger boats have an engine, sink and marine WC (the heads) and the skin (or through-hull) fittings where fluid enters or leaves the boat must have seacocks; these are screwed down or turned to prevent sea water from entering. The seacock has to be opened before pumping in water to flush the heads, and both inlet and outlet seacocks have to be turned off after use.

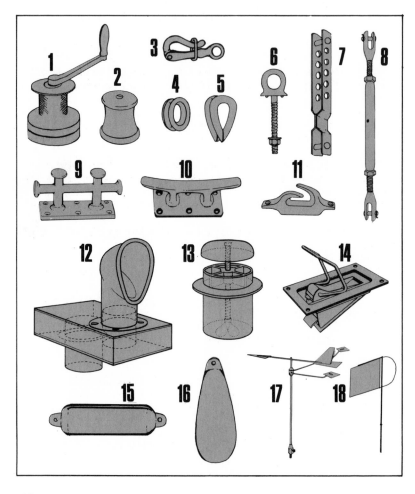

FIGURE 12: MORE CHANDLERY AND GEAR

1. Sheet winch. The handle of this top action winch is inserted above the drum. Many winches have more than one gear and, often, one gear is engaged when the handle is turned clockwise and the other when it is turned anti-clockwise. The crew takes several turns around the drum and pulls in the slack before applying extra power with the handle to sheet the sail home. A riding turn must be avoided; the sheet jams and cannot be eased out when a turn taken earlier rides over one taken later.

2. Snubbing winch with no handle, for dinghies: a ratchet allows it to turn in one direction only.

3. Pelican hook: connects two taut ropes or wires that have to be disconnected quickly, for example to provide an opening or gangway in the guardrail.

4 and 5. Metal or plastics thimbles: spliced into an eye in a rope or worked into a sail to reduce chafe (wear) when the rope is shackled to a fitting, the halyard and sheets to the sail, etc.

6. Eyebolt.

7. Shroud or stay adjuster for a racing dinghy. Tension is increased by passing the bolt through a lower pair of holes and through the thimble spliced into the lower end of the rigging wire.

8. Rigging screw. The barrel, with opposite threads at either end, is turned one way to increase its length and reduce the tension of the rigging wire; turning the barrel the other way increases tension. The lock nuts prevent the rigging screw from working loose, but a wire should also be passed through the central hole and the fork terminals at either end.

9. Crosshead bollard to which mooring ropes are belayed. A heavy fitting for a larger keelboat.

10. Cleat to which a mooring line, halyard, sheet etc is belayed.

11. Fairlead, usually fitted on either side at bow and stern to hold the mooring ropes in place.

12. Dorade ventilator, named after the famous ocean racer for which the first such ventilator was made. The vent pipes are staggered, and the one through which air enters the cabin extends some inches above the deck so that spray taken in through the cowl does not find its way below but drains out through holes in the box fitted round the vents.

13. Mushroom ventilator.

14. Self-bailer for a dinghy: it is lowered when the boat is sailing fast so that water in the bottom of the cockpit is sucked out as she speeds through the water.

15 and 16. Inflatable or foam-filled fenders, hung over the side to protect the topsides from damage. 15 can be hung fore-and-aft or vertically. A pear-shaped fender is essential if a boat has flared topsides.

17. Windex wind direction indicator, fitted at the masthead. Some have phosphorescent reference tabs and vane for use at night.

18. Racing flag, generally very light material kept taut by the wire frame.

FIGURE 13: PARTS OF A SAILING DINGHY

1. Burgee: must fly clear above the truck to show wind direction at the masthead.
2. Main halyard sheave: the main halyard which hoists the mainsail runs over the sheave and down inside the hollow mast.
3. Mast, now almost always aluminium.
4. Groove into which the luff is fed.
5. Tang to which stays and shrouds are shackled.
6. Shroud.
7. Spreaders: hold the shrouds out to improve the angle they make with the mast.
8. Forestay.
9. Forestay tensioner: here a light-weight rigging screw, but may be a tackle or lanyard.
10. Stemhead fitting to which the forestay is attached.
11. Eye through which is led the shock cord that keeps the trapeze wire taut.
12. Foredeck: in light racing dinghies may not support a man's weight.
13. Inspection covers providing access to and ventilation for the buoyancy compartment forward.
14. Sheaves where the internal main and jib halyards emerge from the mast.
15. Shroud adjuster: the bolt passes through the holes and a split ring through the end of the bolt prevents it from working free.
16. Chain plate: anchorage for shrouds.
17. Trapeze: the wire is shackled to a tang high on the mast, the ring at the lower end being slipped over the hook on the trapeze harness worn by the crew who mans the jib sheet while standing out to windward to prevent the boat from heeling.
18. Mast step with rack to allow the mast position to be altered.
19. Jib sheet track with fairlead and jam cleat.
20. Cam cleat and fairlead for the traveller control line.
21. Tiller.
22. Tiller extension, enables the helmsman to steer while sitting out.
23. Side decks incorporating buoyancy tanks.
24. Transom.
25. Hinged transom flap through which water on board can be sucked out when the boat is sailing fast, or drained out on shore.
26. Lifting rudder, raised.
27. Rudder cheeks.
28. Rudder head.
29. Hoist for raising the rudder blade.
30. Swivelling mainsheet ratchet block.
31. Cockpit: the entire undecked area.
32. Toe-straps beneath which the helmsman hooks his feet when sitting out.
33. Traveller which slides on an athwartships track.
34. Boom, grooved to take the foot of the mailsail.
35. Centre mainsheet, rove through blocks.
36. Thwart: stiffens the hull transversely, braces the centreboard case and can be used as a seat.
37. Centreboard case.
38. Centreboard.
39. Hoist for raising the centreboard.

40. Kicking strap rigged as a tackle. Holds the boom down when the mainsheet is eased out.
41. Gooseneck: universal joint which connects the boom to the mast.
42. Topping lift, if fitted.

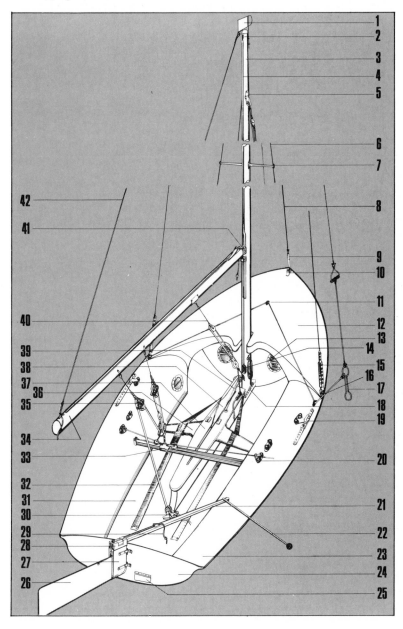

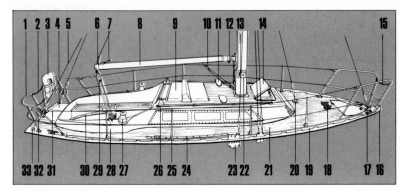

FIGURE 14: A KEELBOAT ABOVE DECKS

1. Stainless steel stern pulpit (or pushpit). Generally a continuous structure .
2. Here the gap amidships makes boarding easier when the boat is moored stern on to the shore. The gap is closed by chain or wire rope.
3. Life-jacket ready to throw to a man who has fallen overboard. More usual is a horseshoe-shaped lifebuoy with a water light attached to mark his position at night.
4. Hatch in the afterdeck, providing access to the afterpeak.
5. Backstay: here the lower part of the backstay divides to distribute the load either side to the quarters.
6. Boom cap to which the topping lift is shackled. The topping lift runs to a point high on the mast and supports the boom when the sail is lowered.
7. Outhaul: adjusts the tension of the foot.
8. Boom, generally anodized aluminium.
9. Sliding hatch over the companionway.
10. Kicking strap. Holds the boom down to prevent the sail from twisting excessively when the mainsheet is eased out.
11. Ventilator cowl: generally pliable plastics which gives when stepped on or if a sheet gets caught beneath it.
12. Roller reefing gear: turns the boom, wrapping the sail around it to reduce the area of sail set.
13. Downhaul: the mainsail is hoisted fully and the halyard cleated before tensioning the luff by pulling down the boom.
14. Watertight forehatch: large enough for the crew to go below or to climb on deck, strong enough to tread on and, usually, translucent to provide light for the fo'c's'le.
15. Pulpit: like the stern pulpit is normally a continuous structure but here has a chain which is removed when boarding.
16. Stemhead fitting: often with a roller over which the anchor cable runs.
17. Forestay with rigging screw.
18. Cleats for the mooring ropes. Just forward of the cleats is the cover to the well in which anchor and cable are stowed.
19. Toe rail: a low wooden or metal rail fitted along the sides to provide a foothold. The holes, scuppers, allow water shipped on deck to flow overboard. Toe rails may also be bolted to the deck further inboard.
20. Inner forestay, or baby stay.
21. Side decks either side of the coachroof and cockpit. To prevent the crew from

slipping on wet decks all decking is either painted with gritty non-slip deck paint or is covered with a material that provides a good foothold.

22. Halyard winch mounted on the mast.

23. Chain plates to which are shackled the rigging screws that tension the shrouds.

24. Track bolted to the side deck so that the headsail sheet lead can be adjusted.

25. Stanchion.

26. Grab rails.

27. Headsail sheet winches.

28. Cockpit coaming: prevents water on deck from flowing into the cockpit.

29. Mainsheet rove through a fiddle block at the boom and through a foot block shackled to the traveller which slides on a track fitted athwartships in the cockpit.

30. Tiller. The rudder post of a keelboat generally passes through the sole (the floor) of the cockpit which is usually watertight or self-draining: any water shipped returns to the sea through drains either side of the sole.

31. Mooring cleat to which mooring ropes are belayed. Above; the rigging screw that tensions the guardrail is connected to the pushpit with a pelican hook so that the guardrail can be opened quickly when required.

32. Backstay tensioner. With these wheel type tensioners the standing rigging can be adjusted while the boat is sailing.

33. Chain plate; the toggle to which the tensioner is attached reduces torsional stress.

FIGURE 15: ACCOMMODATION ON BOARD A CRUISING BOAT

Port is the left hand side looking forward, starboard the right. From forward: a watertight bulkhead separates the chain locker in the forepeak from the forecabin. The vee-shaped berths may be converted into a double berth by inserting a wedge-shaped cushion centrally. Bulkheads and doors close off the area containing a hanging locker to starboard, and the heads (WC) and washing facilities to port. In the main cabin the table is lowered at night to provide a double berth. Some larger boats have pilot berths above the settees, with leeboards along the open side to keep the sleeper in his bunk when the boat heels. The chart table and navigator's equipment is to starboard of the companionway; to port is the galley with sink, stowage racks and a stove, usually gimballed so that it stays horizontal when the boat heels. Two quarter berths extend aft beneath the side decks. The stowage space beside them here is used for clothes, but more often serves as a cockpit locker for ropes, fenders etc. Sail bags can be seen stowed in the sail locker in the afterpeak. The cockpit sole has a large watertight hatch above the engine. Smaller boats may have no chart table, one quarter berth with a cockpit locker on the opposite side and, in the fo'c's'le, either hinged pipe cots or a canvas root berth which is normally rolled out of the way.

Rope and wire rope, splicing and whipping

Just as synthetic materials have largely replaced wood as boat-building materials so have hemp, manila and cotton rope been replaced by cordage made of synthetic fibres. Polyester ropes, sold under trade names such as Terylene, Dacron and Trevira, stretch very little and are suitable for halyards and sheets. Nylon ropes combine great tensile strength with elasticity, characteristics which make them ideal for anchor cables and tow-ropes. Polyethylene and polypropylene ropes are less strong, but because they float they are suitable for mooring ropes, towing water skiers etc. Laid rope is usually made of three strands twisted together, but braided rope with 8 or 16 plaited strands is smoother and pleasanter to handle, and is often preferred for sheets and halyards.

Wire rope is now almost always stainless steel, and its characteristics vary according to its construction. Apart from rod rigging which is a solid extrusion, wire rope is made up of wires twisted into strands which are laid into rope. 1 × 19 (one strand, nineteen wires) is often preferred for standing rigging which is required to stretch as little as possible, but running rigging must be more flexible to pass over a block or sheave and may be of 6 × 7 or 7 × 19 construction.

Splicing is an art that has had to change with the new materials, and different splicing methods are used depending on whether the rope is laid, braided or double braided. Most common are the eye

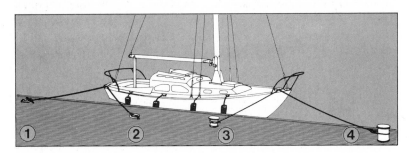

FIGURE 16: MOORING ALONGSIDE

When lying alongside another boat or a pier the boat must be moored so that she stays parallel to the pier without moving forward or aft, and bow and stern must not swing out in reponse to the wind or tidal stream. The springs must lead well forward from a point near the stern, and well aft from a point near the bow. Breast ropes led at right angles to the fore-and-aft line may also be required at bow and stern. 1 stern rope: 2, 3 springs: 4 bow rope.

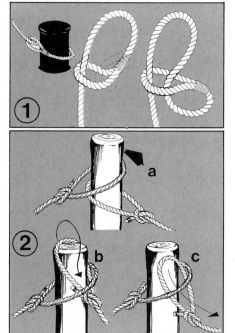

FIGURES 17 and 18:
MOORING ROPES

1. The eye in the end of a mooring rope may be too small to pass over a bollard, but a bigger loop can be made as left.
2. The first boat to moor is often also the first to leave, and another boat's mooring ropes may lie above her own. Instead of untying the other boat and hanging on like grim death to her mooring rope with one hand to prevent her from going adrift while you unhitch your own, pull your boat towards the post until there is enough slack to pass your bowline up through the loop in the other boat's rope and over the top of the post. It will then pull free.

splice with which an eye is formed in the end of a rope, and the rope to wire splice, used to connect a rope tail to a wire sheet or halyard. Wire is rarely spliced manually, nowadays; an eye is often made with the patented Talurit system, the wire being passed twice through a soft metal ferrule which is squeezed tight under pressure to hold the wire strands firmly. A shroud or stay usually has a terminal at top and bottom so that it can be attached to tangs and rigging screws.

Rope ends must be prevented from unlaying, and the fibres of small synthetic ropes can often be welded together by applying heat or a naked flame and rolling them. Larger synthetic ropes and laid ropes are whipped by taking turns around the ends with light twine.

Right   **Wrong**

FIGURE 19: BELAYING

Take a turn under both horns, cross over the cleat and under one horn; repeat and finish with a half hitch. The rope should pass under the further horn first, as in the figure left, to prevent succeeding turns from jamming the rope. The final half hitch should be made so that the end of the rope is held by a part that is crossing the cleat, as left.

Knots, bends, hitches and coiling

There are many methods of belaying a rope on a cleat or making it fast to a bollard, and of securing one rope to another or to some object such as a spar or fitting, but a seaman only uses those knots, bends and hitches that do not slip, jam or come undone when under load, and that can be undone easily when required, even when wet. Many traditional knots prove unsatisfactory when made with smooth nylon and polyester ropes, but those shown in this book can be made with natural or synthetic fibre ropes and are reliable. The safety of boat and crew may well depend on a single knot.

Rope must run out easily when required, and is therefore coiled neatly, ready for use. A heavy mooring rope is coiled more easily if the loops are laid on top of one another on deck, and it is then stowed in a locker where it will not fall overboard or trip up the crew. A halyard is lighter and the loops can be carried in one hand, the coil either being hung on the cleat to which the halyard is belayed or placed in the box provided at the foot of the mast.

The life of rope is shortened if it is allowed to chafe against any object, and a mooring rope, for example, has to be led clear of stanchions and the guardrail so that it will not rub against them when the boat rocks to the wash of passing vessels. The strength of wire rope is reduced if it is allowed to kink, and it must therefore be handled and coiled carefully.

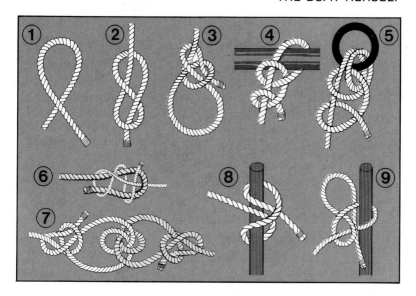

FIGURE 20: KNOTS, BENDS AND HITCHES

1. A loop is made by crossing the end of the rope over the standing part.
2. Figure of eight knot: a stopper knot made in the end of a rope to prevent it from unreeving. Make a loop, pass the end under the standing part and back down through the loop.
3. Bowline: provides a permanent loop with a non-slip knot. Make a small loop slightly further from the end than twice the diameter of the permanent loop required. Pass the end up through the small loop, behind the standing part and down through the small loop.
4. A rope can be made fast quickly but temporarily by making two half hitches around the standing part; they slip along the standing part and are pulled tight to the rail.
5. Fisherman's bend: take a round turn, passing the rope through the ring twice; make a half hitch, passing the end round the standing part and through the turn, pull tight and finish with a half hitch. Often recommended for bending the cable to the anchor but may come undone when the cable drags on the sea-bed. Always shackle the cable to the anchor.
6. Double sheet bend: connects two ropes of different sizes but, like the single sheet bend, may slip when made with synthetic fibre rope, so use …
7. Two bowlines. The two small loops limit play and reduce chafe.
8. Clove hitch. A useful hitch that is satisfactory unless the diameter of the bollard or of the rope is excessive because the hitch will not then jam itself and can pull free.
9. A slipped end to a knot is sometimes advisable; a strong tug on the end of the line releases the knot quickly, even when it is under load.

Auxiliary engines

Not so long ago engines were spurned by sailors, but traffic everywhere has increased so much that they have become not merely acceptable but essential. In busy waters where there are so many boats nearby that a sailing boat cannot manoeuvre freely, she may only be able to reach a destination to windward if she starts her engine, and many marinas and small harbours are laid out in such a way that it is impossible to get into the berths when under sail. Another advantage is that the crew can enjoy the convenience of electric lighting because the engine charges the batteries.

Outboard engines

If there is too little space to instal an inboard engine complete with gearbox and shafting, the only answer is an outboard. A portable single unit houses engine, gears, shafting and propeller, and is usually clamped to the stern. It can be tilted to raise the propeller clear of the water when approaching the shore or to reduce resistance when under sail. The power output of outboards varies from 2–200 hp, 1·5–150 kW, and they have a higher power to weight ratio (the ratio of the output of the engine in hp or kW to its weight in lbs or kgs) than inboard engines, but there are disadvantages.

An outboard cannot be clamped directly to a transom raked well forward or aft and normally, only two shaft lengths are available, the standard length being $14^{1}/_{2}$ in (37 cm). Even with the long shaft, 20in (51 cm) long, the propeller may not be immersed sufficiently deeply; it then races and causes engine wear. When the rudder is hung on the transom the outboard has to be clamped to one side, and if the engine is used to help the boat beat to windward the propeller is lifted clear of the water when she heels to one side but is too deeply immersed when she heels to the other side. The propeller is sometimes lowered by shipping the outboard in a well near the stern, but the engine rarely performs efficiently because of inadequate ventilation; the air taken in is often also fouled by the exhaust.

There is another major disadvantage to using an outboard to propel a keelboat. Outboards are designed for light, fast motor boats and have small propellers that rotate at high speed, but for a keelboat a relatively large propeller that rotates slowly is required to convert

FIGURE 21: ENGINE AND TRANSMISSION

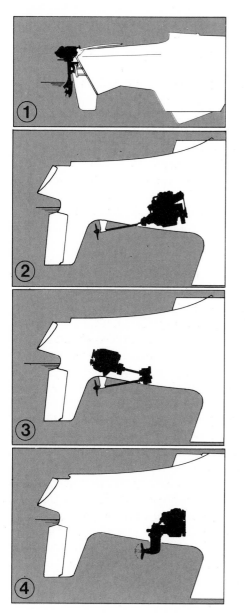

1. Outboard engine, usually clamped to a bracket near the transom but sometimes shipped in a well aft.
2. Conventional straight shafting with drive shaft, gearbox and propeller shaft aligned.
3. Vee-drive: drive shaft and propeller shaft run forward to meet at an acute angle at the gearbox, and they rotate in opposite directions. This lay-out may be preferable because there is more space aft, or because the boat's trim is improved with the heavy engine further aft.
4. Sail drive: the engine drives the propeller shaft through two bevel gears at either end of the vertical shaft that passes through the hull. Sail drive was developed from the inboard-outboard (or outdrive) which is an inboard engine installed close by the stern, coupled to a transmission unit like that of an outboard.

as much as possible of the engine's output into thrust. The unsatisfactory combination of high propeller speed and small diameter is evident from the following figures which show how many hp or kW are required for every 2,200 lbs or tonne of boat weight:

- Inboard: 4 hp or 3 kW
- Outboard: 9·5 hp or 7 kW

Thus the largest boat that can be propelled effectively by a 15 hp or 11 kW outboard weighs about 3,300 lbs or 1·5 tonnes, and an outboard is therefore not an attractive proposition for boats over about 23 ft (7 m) in length.

Inboard engines

The choice here lies between petrol or diesel engines. From the safety aspect the diesel is undoubtedly preferable because diesel fuel has a much lower flash point than petrol. The absence of an ignition system also eliminates a further cause of explosion. Diesels are robust and require relatively little maintenance, but they are considerably more expensive, larger, heavier and noisier. Although the greater risk of fire and explosion with a petrol engine can be reduced by careful installation of the engine, fuel lines and petrol tank, it cannot be eliminated. Petrol engines are also less reliable because of ignition problems caused by damp and salt water which corrode the contacts.

Transmission is almost always mechanical, and the gearbox generally has reverse and reduction gears. The latter reduces high engine rotational rate to a lower rate suitable for the propeller. When the propeller rotates in one direction the boat makes headway and sails forward. But if reverse gear is then engaged the propeller rotates in the opposite direction – she slows and stops – the boat first loses way and then makes sternway, moving stern first.

As to propellers, those with two blades are preferable to those with three because resistance is lower. Folding propellers are popular because the blades fold to lie fore-and-aft when sailing, but they are less efficient and are relatively ineffective in astern gear. With variable pitch propellers the pitch (the angle of the blade to the water) can be varied to suit different loads and speeds. The blades can also be turned to produce thrust in the reverse direction, eliminating the need for a reverse gear, but this mechanism is rather vulnerable to damage.

Wind and water

A sailing boat, designed to float in water and to be propelled through it by wind power, is completely dependent on these two elements. She cannot make way under sail if there is no wind, she will be aground if the water is too shallow, and she may be endangered if the wind is too strong and the waves too high, or if she is swept onto a shoal by a fast-running tidal stream.

Wind

Before going for a sail the skipper has to consider the speed and direction of the wind. From the meteorological office or from shipping and weather forecasts broadcast on the radio, the skipper obtains information as to what winds are expected, but forecasts may prove to be wrong because conditions can and do change extremely rapidly. Local factors also affect winds considerably, and the crew therefore keep a good look-out for wind shifts by checking their visible effects on boats sailing some distance to windward, and by watching flags or smoke on shore.

The Beaufort scale, (pp 110–112) used to indicate wind strength, grades winds according to speed into 13 forces from force 0, calm, to force 12, hurricane. A freshening wind becomes stronger, and one that moderates blows less hard. If the wind is gusty there are temporary spells of much fresher wind, while a lull is a relatively short period of lighter wind. Wind direction is given as the point of the compass from which it blows, and a wind that shifts to blow from a direction further clockwise is said to veer whereas a backing wind shifts anti-clockwise. Thus the forecast may talk of force 4 south-westerly winds, backing to south and freshening to force 6. Fluky winds are generally light and vary considerably in direction.

The general direction and strength of wind depends on the position of areas of high and low pressure. A high pressure area or anticyclone is usually slow-moving with relatively settled weather and winds, while fast-moving low pressure areas or depressions are associated with strong winds and the major wind shifts that accompany warm and cold fronts. Local land and sea breezes result from the difference in temperature between land and sea; the sea breeze blows from cooler sea to warmer land during the day, and is replaced at night by the land breeze which blows seaward when the sea is warmer than the land.

WELCOME ON BOARD

The sailor refers to a head wind or a foul wind when it blows from the direction towards which he intends to sail, a fair wind or a free wind when it is favourable, a beam wind when it blows at right angles to his course, and a following wind when it blows from astern. A wind that frees is one that shifts to blow from a direction nearer the stern, but if it heads it blows from nearer the bow. Strength and direction are affected by objects such as mountains, trees or sails lying in the wind's path and, when racing, a boat with a clear wind, undisturbed by the sails of other boats or obstacles nearby, will sail faster than one suffering from a dirty wind. To blanket a boat is to take the wind from her sails.

Tides and tidal streams

If there is no wind at all, a boat floats in the water without moving through it, but the whole body of water may be moving and in this case the boat will drift over the ground, carried downstream by a river current or along the coast by a tidal stream; she may only be able to return to her departure point under engine or if a motor-boat offers her a tow. She may also set sail safely and return some hours later to find that the tide has ebbed and that she cannot return to shore because the water has become so shallow that she will run aground or be stove in by some underwater obstruction.

In British coastal waters there are two tides each day. Sea level is highest at high water, (HW), falls during the ebb to reach its lowest level at low water (LW) about six hours later, and then rises during the flood until HW which occurs again after another six hours. The stand is the period at HW and LW when water level stays virtually constant. The range of a tide is the difference between the height of the water at HW and its height at LW. Range is least at neap tides and then increases gradually for about a week when spring tides occur, after which range decreases again until neaps. At springs the level of water is higher at HW and lower at LW than it is at HW and LW neaps (see Fig 22, p. 32).

Tidal streams flow in response to the vertical rise and fall of the tide, and the rate at which they flow is greatest at springs and least at neaps. The flood stream sets into harbours and estuaries, and along the coast, generally for about six hours. After slack water the ebb stream starts to flow in the reverse direction and again is followed by slack water some six hours later at the turn of the tide. The times of HW and LW rarely coincide with those of slack water.

Just as the tidal stream often flows at maximum rate during the third and fourth hours after slack water, so is the rate of rise and fall of water level often greatest during the third and fourth hours of ebb and flood tide, but there are many local exceptions such as in the Solent where there are two high waters and only one low water in every tidal cycle.

The predicted times and heights of HW and LW are listed daily in tide tables, and are often displayed on harbour or sailing club notice boards. The set and rate of tidal streams at hourly intervals is given in a tidal stream atlas and in chartlets printed in *Reeds Nautical Almanac*. Given this information, the skipper can allow for set when crossing a tidal stream, or use a fair tidal stream to help him towards his destination instead of being frustrated by a foul tidal stream which may be so strong that the boat can do no more than stem the tide, making no progress over the ground until the rate slackens.

Waves

The height of waves raised by the wind increases with the strength of the wind and with fetch, which is the distance that wind blows over open water. Waves that persist after the wind that raised them has dropped are termed swell. Tidal streams also affect seas, which are smaller and easier when the wind is blowing towards the direction in which the tidal stream sets, but become shorter and more awkward when the tidal stream turns to set in the opposite direction. Seas are particularly vicious in races or tide-rips; these are marked on charts and are best avoided. Long seas are relatively easy to take but a boat often pounds in short, steep seas, losing way as the bow slams down on them. A confused sea that is caused by a change in the direction of the wind makes the motion of a boat extremely uncomfortable because she pitches and rolls without any rhythmic pattern. The Beaufort scale given on pp. 110–112 includes a description of the seas raised offshore by winds varying from force 0–12.

Depth of water

A landlubber might imagine at high water that a shallow centreboard dinghy could sail safely wherever he could see water, but sandbanks, rocks and wrecks may be revealed at low water. On non-tidal inland lakes and reservoirs water level changes little and local sailors know where the dangers are. In tidal waters sea level changes continuously. Many of the figures printed on charts are soundings which indicate the depth of water at that place below a reference level which is called chart datum. On British metric charts covering tidal waters, chart datum is LAT, Lowest Astronomical Tide, and sea level rarely falls lower. Actual depth at a place in tidal waters varies with the state of the tide; if the tide tables predict heights for the day of 3 metres above LAT at HW and 0.8 metres at LW, the actual depth of water at a place where the sounding is 2.4 metres is predicted to be 5.4 metres at HW and 3.2 metres at LW.

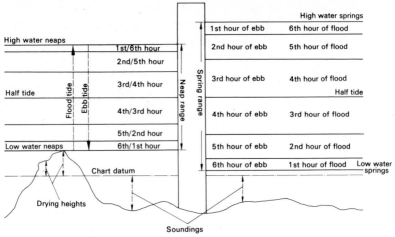

FIGURE 22: TIDES

Height of tide is given above a reference level, chart datum, which is Lowest Astronomical Tide on British metric charts (Mean Low Water Springs on older fathom charts). Soundings are given in metres below LAT and heights of features that dry (visible when water level is at chart datum) are given above LAT. Heights of features that are permanently above sea level are given above Mean High Water Springs.

In many UK waters the twelfths rule applies to the rise and fall of tides. Divide range by 12: in the first and sixth hours of flood and ebb sea level rises or falls one-twelfth, in the second and fifth two-twelfths, in the third and fourth three-twelfths. There are many local exceptions.

Sailing and helming

Directions and alterations of course are often referred to by the wind direction because wind is all-important to a sailing boat. Leeward and lee refer to objects and directions that are downwind, such as lee shore, leeway, leeward boat, whereas windward and weather refer to objects and directions towards the wind, such as weather gunwale and windward mark. When altering course the helmsman either bears away or luffs up. To bear away he puts the helm up, pulling the tiller to windward so that the bows turn to leeward, away from the wind, and the crew ease out the sheets. To luff up he puts the helm down, pushing the tiller to leeward so that the bows turn towards the wind, and the crew harden the sheets to bring the sails closer to the centreline.

Anyone can understand why a boat sails downwind – the wind thrusts her forward by pushing on the sail, just as it blows a piece of paper away – but many non-sailors are surprised to find that a boat can sail towards the wind. No boat can advance under sail when she is pointing directly towards the wind or if the helmsman heads into a sector of roughly 90° (45° to either side of the wind direction); she will be driven backwards and will make sternway. Slow cruising boats can rarely sail closer than about 45° to the wind, but a well-tuned racing boat may point considerably higher. (Fig 24).

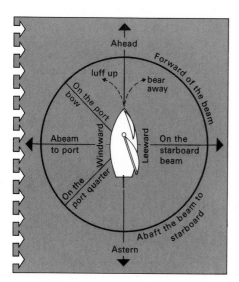

FIGURE 23: DIRECTIONS

Windward is towards the direction from which the wind is blowing, and the opposite is leeward. Starboard relates to all that is inside or outside the boat, on the right-hand side of the centreline when looking towards the bow: the opposite is port. Fine on the bow is between on the bow and ahead, broad on the bow between on the bow and abeam; fine on the quarter is between on the quarter and astern, broad on the quarter is between on the quarter and abeam. This boat is on port tack.

The aerodynamics and hydrodynamics of sailing are far too advanced and complicated for this book but, to put it as simply as possible, the wind, blowing at this angle of 45° or so to the centreline, thrusts on the sail and tries to push the boat sideways; when wind pressure is transmitted to the long, narrow underwater body, the lateral plane (bottom, keel or centreboard and rudder) opposes sideways movement and the boat therefore moves forward, taking the line of least resistance. The sails help her to do so because pressure is lower on the lee side of the sails, and this draws her towards the wind.

A boat is said to be on port tack when the wind comes from port; boom and mainsail lie to starboard of the centreline. She is on starboard tack when the wind strikes the starboard side of the boat first; the sails are then sheeted to port.

When pointing close to the wind, with sails sheeted in close to the centreline, a boat is said to be close-hauled or on the wind. When an objective lies directly to windward, she beats towards it, sailing a zigzag course, close-hauled first on one tack, then on the other which

FIGURE 24: POINTS OF SAILING

The white arrows show the true wind's direction and the black arrows that of the apparent wind which results from true wind and boat speed. The top two boats are close-hauled, but the lower of the two is sailing faster and not pointing so close to the true wind. The faster that a boat sails the more does the direction of the apparent wind vary from that of the true wind; a very fast catamaran, for example, will be sailing at an angle of roughly 45° to the apparent wind; with her sails hardened right in, when she is heading roughly at right angles to the true wind. The third boat has borne away to a close reach and her sails have been eased out. The apparent wind is blowing at right angles to the centreline of the fourth boat which is on a beam reach. The fifth and sixth boats, broad reaching and running respectively, have borne away further, the sheets have been eased out again and the spinnaker has been hoisted. All the boats are on starboard tack with the wind striking the starboard side of the boat first (cf Fig 23, boat on port tack).

Typical boat speeds are shown by the curve on the right. She works to windward best when sailing at about 45° to the true wind, and her speed drops drastically if the helmsman pinches to sail at an angle of 38°. Her fastest course is roughly at right angles to the true wind when she makes about 5·5 knots, but her speed decreases as she bears away and she makes only 75–85% of her maximum speed when running.

is roughly at right angles to the first, until the objective is reached. The helmsman changes tack by going about or tacking; he luffs up and swings the bows through the eye of the wind and round on to the opposite tack.

If the helmsman of a close-hauled boat bears away progressively while the crew ease out the sheets she first sails on a close reach, then on a beam reach with the wind abeam, then on a broad reach with a quartering wind and finally on a run with a following wind and the sails eased right out until the boom is almost at right angles to the centreline. If the helmsman then bears away still further, the boat will change tacks by gybing, the sail and boom slamming over to the opposite side as the stern swings through the wind.

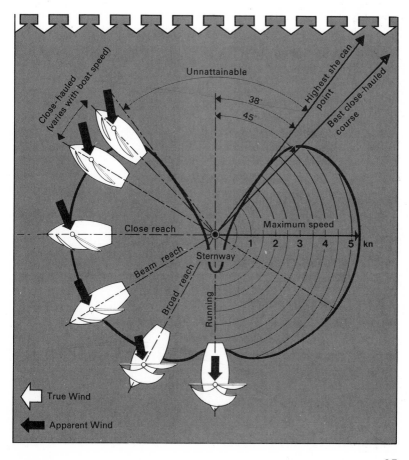

True wind and apparent wind

People who are standing on a boat lying motionless at anchor feel the atmospheric wind that is blowing, and this is called the true wind. But suppose that it is dead calm – they cannot feel a breath of wind – and that the engine is then started so that the boat gathers way to make, say, 3 knots. Immediately the crew will feel a 3-knot wind blowing from dead ahead. This wind results entirely from boat speed.

When the boat is making way under sail its crew again feel a wind on their faces and this, the apparent wind that propels the boat, results from the combined effects of true wind and the wind caused by boat speed. The direction and speed of the apparent wind differ from those of the true wind, and the faster a boat sails the greater is this difference. When a boat is on a run the true and apparent winds both blow from dead astern, but on all other points of sailing the apparent wind blows from nearer the bow, and its direction is shown by the burgee, flag or vane at the masthead. When the true wind is blowing at an angle of about 110° to the centreline, true and apparent wind speeds are much the same, but when the boat luffs up from that course the apparent wind becomes progressively stronger, whereas as she bears away apparent wind speed decreases to become least when she is running. On a run the difference between true wind speed and apparent wind speed is the speed at which the boat is moving over the ground.

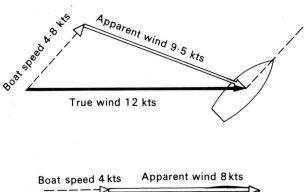

FIGURE 24A: TRUE AND APPARENT WIND

Rule of the road

The water has to be shared with many other craft, and the only way to avoid collisions is to keep a proper look-out, to know the rules of the road that are in force and to abide by them. In British and many other waters these rules are the *International Regulations for Preventing Collisions at Sea*, and they specify the action that both boats must take when there is a risk of collision. They may be summarised as follows:

- A sailing vessel is defined as being propelled only by wind on her sails. If her engine is running as well she ranks as power-driven.
- When two vessels are on collision courses the boat that has to keep clear alters course and/or speed; the other stays on her original course and does not alter speed.
- Two boats sailing on opposite tacks: the boat on port tack must keep clear of the boat on starboard tack.
- Two boats on the same tack: the boat to windward must keep clear of the boat to leeward.
- A port tack boat may see another approaching from windward but cannot see if she is on port or starboard tack. The port tack boat keeps clear.
- Overtaking: any vessel overtaking another must keep clear.
- Two power-driven boats meeting head-on or nearly head-on: both alter course to starboard.
- Two power-driven vessels crossing: the boat that sees the other approaching from starboard keeps clear (at night she sees the other boat's red port light).
- When a boat under sail meets a power-driven vessel it is normally the power-driven vessel that has to keep clear, for example a motor boat or a sailing boat using her auxiliary engine keeps clear of a boat under sail. There are, however, many occasions when a sailing boat should take action in good time to prevent the situation arising where the power-driven vessel has to give way. Sailing boats should avoid the waters used by larger vessels, and should not cause commercial or naval vessels to alter course unnecessarily. Large ships are far less handy and often draw so much water that they have to stay in a channel deepened by dredging (vessels constrained by their draft). A 10,000-ton vessel takes about five minutes to lose all way, and a large tanker can cover as much as two miles during the 20 minutes that she may need to come to a stop. A sailing boat also has to keep clear of other classes of power-driven vessels that

FIGURE 25: RULE OF THE ROAD

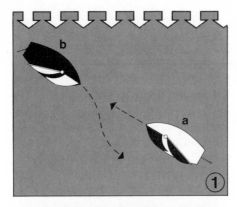

1. Port tack (b) keeps clear of starboard tack (a).

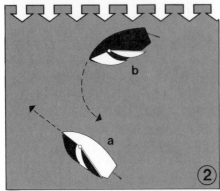

2. Windward boat (b) keeps clear of leeward boat (a).

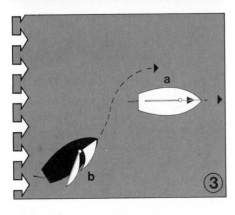

3. Overtaking boat (b) keeps clear.

manoeuvre with difficulty, such as fishing boats with nets out, cable-layers and minesweepers, as well as those that are not under command (uncontrollable).

When two boats are on collision courses their relative bearings do

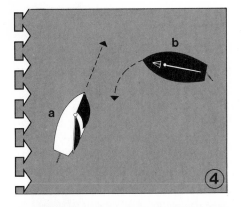

4. Power-driven vessel (b) keeps clear of sailing vessel (a)

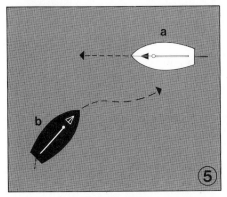

5. Power-driven vessels crossing: boat (b) sees the other to starboard and keeps clear.

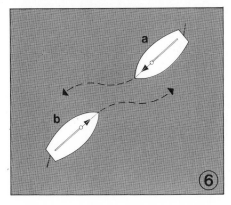

6. Power-driven vessels meeting head-on: both alter course to starboard.

not change. For example, the helmsman of a sailing boat may see a coaster in line with the boat's starboard shroud, and a few minutes later while sitting in the same position, he sees her in line with the stanchion nearer the bow. The relative bearing has then changed and the coaster will cross safely ahead. On the other hand if the coaster is still in line with the shroud the relative bearings have not changed although the boats are closer together than before, and if the sailing boat is using her engine the helmsman must alter course to avoid a collision (power-driven vessels crossing). but if she is being propelled by wind alone it is the coaster that must keep clear.

It is generally preferable to pass astern of a boat when keeping clear, and any alteration of course must be so obvious that the other boat understands what is intended. Although the boat with right of way is required to maintain her course and speed, the other boat may fail to give way, and the right of way boat must then take whatever action is appropriate to avoid a collision.

More details of the rule of the road are on pp. 102–104.

A short sail

The crew of the boat do not simply step aboard and sail away: they must make much more preparation than say, for a car journey. For a start they must be wearing enough clothes for warmth and shoes or boots with non-slip soles so that they do not lose their footing. They need to take waterproof clothing to keep themselves dry, and more clothes to change into if they are going sailing for more than a few hours. A shackle spanner or marline spike is also needed for tightening up and undoing shackles, and is often combined with a pocket knife with a lanyard to go around the waist.

A dinghy is often transported to the water's edge on a trailer towed behind a car, or from a dinghy park by trolley, and the mast may have to be stepped and the standing rigging set up before the sails can be bent on. A keelboat may be moored or anchored some distance from the shore, and the crew then row or motor out to her

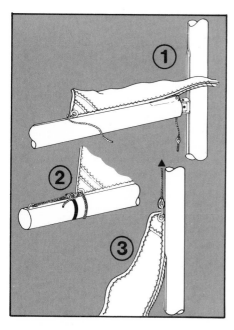

FIGURE 26: BENDING ON AND HOISTING THE MAINSAIL

Slip the battens into their pockets. 1. Feed the foot rope into the boom groove, secure the tack to the gooseneck with a shackle or lashing and 2. pull out the foot with the outhaul, perhaps lashing it to the boom. The clew must not be pulled beyond the black band when racing. 3. Shackle the halyard to the head, top up the boom with the topping lift (if any), feed the luff rope into the mast groove as the sail is hoisted, having checked that the mainsheet is uncleated and running freely. Tension the luff and cleat the halyard, unless there is a downhaul in which case cleat the halyard first and then pull down the boom. Slack off the topping lift. Alternatively the sail may be laced to the spars or have slides sewn to the foot and luff which run on tracks on the boom and mast.

41

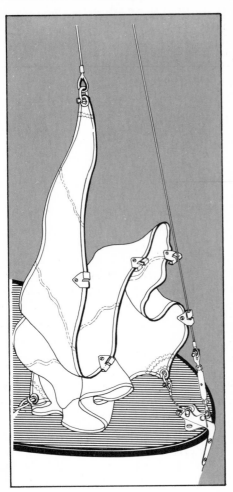

FIGURE 27 BENDING ON AND HOISTING THE HEADSAIL

Shackle the tack to the stemhead fitting and the jib halyard to the head after checking that the halyard is clear of the standing rigging. Snap the hanks on to the forestay and attach the sheets to the clew either with a shackle or in a dinghy preferably, with a knot. Reeve the sheets through the blocks or fairleads and tie a figure of eight knot in the end. Check that the lead is correct; jib sheets are often led inboard of the shrouds and genoa sheets outboard. When hoisting the headsail swig or winch the halyard really taut before cleating it so that the luff will not sag to leeward when the sail fills.

in a dinghy or tender.

The crew confirm that all the gear needed is on board and in working order. When bending on the sails, they check that the halyards run clear of the standing rigging, that the sheets are correctly led through the fairleads and blocks, with stopper knots in the ends to prevent them from unreeving and, before hoisting the sails, they check that the sheets are not cleated or snarled, in order that the sails can shake freely without filling with wind.

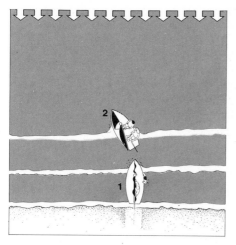

FIGURE 28: LEAVING A BEACH, ONSHORE WIND

1. Hoist the sails, pull the boat into deeper water, lower the centreboard part way. The crew shoves the boat forward hard and scrambles aboard. 2. The helmsman lowers the rudder and puts up the helm. The sails are sheeted in and the centreboard is lowered fully. Speed is essential to avoid being blown straight back on shore. In surf the crew times his shove to coincide with the moment when water runs offshore after a wave has broken on the beach.

Getting under way

The skipper's plans for getting under way depend largely on the wind direction, which is often shown by a burgee or flag hoisted to the masthead. The mainsail can only be hoisted when the wind is forward of the beam, and it is best if the stern is free to swing because the boat will then lie head to wind automatically and the sail will flutter like a flag instead of filling with wind.

There are no problems when leaving a beach if the wind is offshore, blowing from land to sea. The crew holds the boat by the bow, the sails are hoisted, the rudder is shipped and is lowered if the water is deep enough. The crew shoves the bow away from the wind and climbs on board, the sails fill and the centreboard is lowered as the boat sails away. With an onshore wind the crew has to drag the boat into deeper water, as in figure 28, or paddle her offshore and moor her to a post or buoy while the mainsail is hoisted.

Formerly, keelboats too would normally get under way under sail, but a berth or mooring is now generally left under engine power, and in marinas or busy harbours there is often no alternative to this. A sailor should nevertheless be able to leave and return to a berth under sail – after all, the engine could fail to start, or break down.

A boat that is anchored or moored to a buoy will often lie head to wind, and is then said to be wind-rode; both mainsail and headsail can be hoisted, and the headsail is thrust out to one side by hand, say to port. The bow will then pay off to starboard when the mooring buoy is dropped or the anchor is weighed. Sometimes the boat is

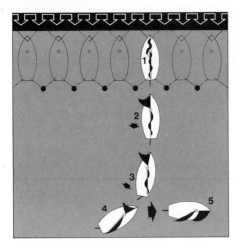

FIGURE 29: LEAVING A PIER OR PONTOON OFFSHORE WIND

Light steady winds only. Uncleat the sheets and check that they are clear to run freely. 1. Hoist the sails, cast off the bow ropes and haul the boat aft with the stern ropes, keeping her head to wind. When clear of the posts 2. back the jib, 3. put the helm down, 4. harden the mainsail and 5. sheet the headsail to leeward. In fluky or stronger winds drop her astern and moor to a post with a bow rope ready to slip (both ends on board) before hoisting sail.

tide-rode, that is, she lies head to tidal stream, often with the wind abeam or on the quarter. She then leaves under headsail alone, sails to where she has ample searoom and is luffed head to wind so that the mainsail can be hoisted.

If the boat is moored alongside to a pier or pontoon it is easiest to get under way when there is an offshore wind; all mooring ropes except the bow rope are removed, the stern swings downwind, the sails are hoisted and the bow is thrust to leeward so that the sails fill as she bears away. A boat may be boxed in by other boats close either side, or the wind may be blowing onshore, and it is then often a case of manhandling her clear, hauling her to a post or buoy offshore with a warp (line) or, perhaps, running out an anchor in the

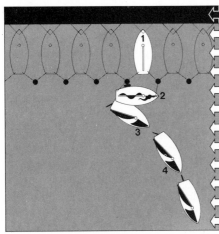

FIGURE 30: LEAVING A PIER, WIND PARALLEL TO THE SHORE

1. Haul the boat aft and clear of the posts, 2. mooring her head to wind. Hoist the sails and 3. shove off hard forward, putting the tiller to windward. 4. Harden in the sheets and sail away.

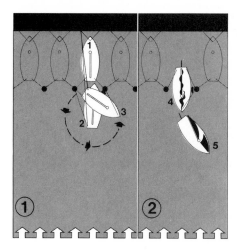

FIGURE 31: LEAVING A PIER, ONSHORE WIND

Motor out stern first. If no engine, light winds only: pass a long mooring rope round a bollard on shore, ready to slip. 1. Haul the boat aft and clear of the posts, 2. heave the stern round 180° with the long rope, 3. keep her head to wind between the posts and 4. hoist the sails quickly. Pull her forward with a mighty heave on both stern ropes. 5. sheeting in the sails rapidly as soon as her head pays off. Smart crewing is essential, and all mooring ropes must slip without catching or she will be forced onto the posts. In stronger winds warp her to a buoy offshore or run out an anchor astern in the dinghy.

dinghy and dropping it some way offshore so that she can be hauled out to lie to it head to wind. If the crew try to hoist a mainsail when the boat is beam on or stern on to the wind, only the onlookers will be amused, and damage may well result because, as soon as the crew starts hoisting, the wind fills the sail and pushes the boat onto the pier or into other boats. It is clear, then, that the way you leave a berth needs to be thought out carefully in advance!

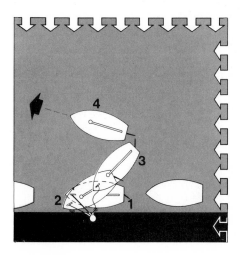

FIGURE 32: LEAVING A PIER UNDER ENGINE, WIND BETWEEN ONSHORE AND DEAD ASTERN

1. Cast off all mooring ropes except a bow rope ready to slip; provide a stout fender for the bow. Put the helm over, turning the rudder towards the shore. Motor slow ahead until the stern has swung out 15–20°. Engine in neutral. 2. Turn the rudder away from the shore, slip the bow rope and motor slow astern. 3. When far enough off shore motor ahead into open water to hoist the sails.

45

Under way, helming and sail trimming

Close-hauled and beating: with the wind blowing at an angle of about 45° to the centreline the sails are hardened right in, and the sheets of a keelboat are cleated. Dinghy sheets are often held by the crew so that the sails can be trimmed or let fly instantly, but may be jammed in a cam jam cleat from which they can be released immediately with an upward jerk. The helmsman has to keep the boat sailing fast and close to the wind, which varies continuously in direction and strength. If he points too high the headsail lifts (the wind blows on its lee side near the luff, pushing it to windward and causing it to shake), but if he is off the wind, that is, if he is not pointing as high as he should be, airflow separates and the sail generates less driving force. He checks that he is pointing close enough by luffing up gently from time to time until the jib just starts to lift, and then bears away just enough to fill the sail.

When close-hauled or beating towards an objective to windward, the helmsman has to choose between sailing too close to the wind and sailing too free. If he pinches, pointing really close to the wind with sheets hardened in as far as possible, the boat sails slower and makes considerably more leeway; if he bears away and sheets are eased slightly she will sail faster but make less ground to windward and that is the direction in which he wants to go. The right compromise has to be found for each boat; some boats work to windward better when pointing higher and sailing slower, others reach an objective more quickly when footing faster, even though they cover a greater distance.

A dinghy sails faster when upright, and the helmsman and crew therefore put their weight to windward to counter wind pressure on the sails. The centreboard is lowered fully when close-hauled.

Reaching: except when close-hauled, the helmsman can head directly towards his destination and he normally steers a straight course; however when broad reaching in a high quartering sea the boat yaws to either side of her course as a wave passes beneath her, and it is better to help her over the seas instead of fighting her and trying to sail absolutely straight.

The crew trim the sails to match the course, easing out the sheets until the luffs just start to lift. They then harden the sails in a fraction until they fill. A good crew checks in this way repeatedly because wind direction changes so often and, if the sail is hardened in too far, the sail produces less drive.

As the boat bears away and the boom is eased out further for a broad reach or a run, the pull of the mainsheet becomes horizontal

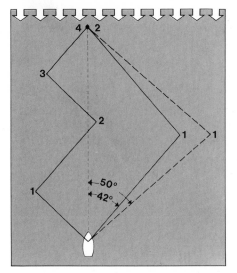

FIGURE 33: BEATING

Both boats are beating towards an objective dead to windward. The boat on the right sails two long legs and only goes about once. Provided that wind direction remains constant she should reach her destination before the boat on the left, which goes about three times sailing two shorter tacks on port and two on starboard, because going about takes time. The two righthand tracks show how performance varies from boat to boat. A faster boat, sailing at an angle of 50° to the wind and following the broken line, sails about 18% further than the other slower boat which sails at 42° to the wind, but both reach their objective at the same time.

rather than vertical, and the boom can therefore lift, allowing the sail to twist excessively, again with a loss of drive. Most boats have a kicking strap to prevent the boom from lifting and, if it is to be effective when the mainsheet is eased out, the kicking strap must be pulled really taut while the boat is head to wind after hoisting the mainsail.

Crew weight is used to keep the boat level and is generally placed slightly further aft than when close-hauled. The centreboard is down on a close reach, partly raised on a beam reach and raised a little further on a broad reach.

Running: when the wind is dead aft the mainsail is eased right out with the boom almost at right angles to the centreline and touching the lee shroud. The headsail, blanketed by the mainsail, cannot fill with wind and is usually lowered if a spinnaker is set. Alternatively it can be sheeted to windward and is either held out by hand in a small boat, or boomed out with the jib stick of a larger dinghy or with the spinnaker pole. The centreboard is normally raised fully to reduce frictional resistance, and the crew of a dinghy usually sit on opposite sides to keep her level.

On a run, the helmsman needs to concentrate. Not only does the boat roll from side to side, sometimes so violently that boom and spinnaker pole dip alternately into the water, but it is all too easy for him to bear away slightly too far, especially in a high following sea.

The boat is then running by the lee, with the wind blowing from a direction to leeward of the centreline, and the probable consequence is an accidental gybe. The boom and mainsail slam over unexpectedly to the opposite side and, in strong winds, can cause damage, injure the crew or capsize a dinghy. In a keelboat an accidental gybe can be prevented by rigging a foreguy, leading forward from the end of the boom to the foredeck.

It is often preferable and can be quicker to tack downwind, sailing first on one broad reach, then gybing and sailing on the other broad reach. The boat sails faster, rolls less violently and there is no fear of an accidental gybe.

FIGURE 34: GOING ABOUT, OR TACKING

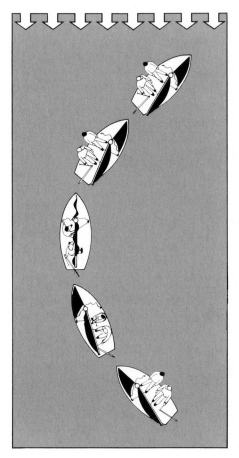

A boat must not lose way when tacking because she will then either stop in irons, head to wind with sails shaking, or miss stays and pay off on the original tack. The helmsman puts the helm down gradually instead of jerking the rudder right over when it would act as a brake and slow her. As she goes about the mainsail swings over automatically, and the crew lets the headsail sheet fly when the sail stops drawing. He does not harden it in to leeward until the boat has paid off on the new tack. Dinghy crews shift their weight to the opposite side when the boom is amidships and the boat head to wind.

A dinghy loses way very quickly and is put about smartly so that she gathers full way again with the minimum of delay, but a heavier keelboat carries her way much further and if she is put about slowly, will shoot some distance to windward while tacking. In smooth seas a boat shoots quite some distance, but in short steep seas she slams on the waves and stops quickly. The helmsman therefore waits for a relatively quiet patch in which to tack, and the crew stands by to back the headsail to help her head round if need be.

Tacking and gybing

Co-ordination between helmsman and crew is essential when changing tacks, especially in larger boats. The helmsman warns the crew of his intention to tack or go about with the words, 'Ready about', and the crew uncleats the headsail sheet. The helmsman says, 'Lee-o' when he puts down the tiller, the boat starts to turn towards the wind, and the crew let the sheet fly as soon as the sail stops drawing, but wait until the bows have swung well past the eye of the wind and on to the new tack before hardening in the headsail again. If the crew sheets in too soon the sail will back and prevent the boat from paying off on the new tack. In a keelboat with a large overlapping genoa one of the crew may go forward to help it round to leeward before returning to the cockpit to help winch in the sheet.

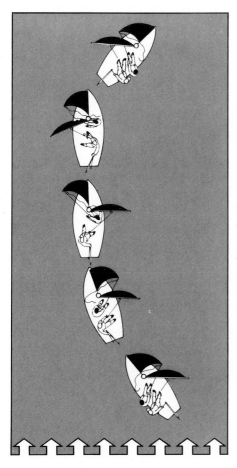

FIGURE 35: GYBING

The helmsman bears away until the boat is running dead before the wind, and the crew hardens in the mainsheet to bring the boom amidships. The helm is put up gently, boom and sail swing over to the other side, and the mainsheet is eased out at lightning speed while the helmsman keeps the boat sailing straight downwind, checking her tendency to luff up sharply when the sail swings over. He often has to apply counter rudder to prevent her broaching, especially in a fresh wind, and the crew must let the mainsheet run right out. Once the boat is sailing steadily downwind the sheet can be hardened and the boat luffed up to whatever course is desired.

A dinghy can be gybed all standing: instead of hardening in the mainsheet the helmsman reaches up and grasps all the parts of the sheet, pulling the sail over from one side to the other. Smaller keelboats can also be gybed all standing when the wind is light.

The warning given before gybing is usually, 'Stand by to gybe'. The crew hardens in the mainsail and, when the helmsman says, 'Gybe-o' and puts the tiller up, the boom swings over. The crew immediately lets the mainsail run right out as quickly as possible and the helmsman applies counter helm, putting the tiller over to the opposite side to prevent the boat from luffing up. If the mainsheet is snarled and does not run out freely the boat will broach, luffing up uncontrollably in stronger winds. Gybing smoothly requires practice and is best learned in lighter breezes. Dinghies are often gybed all standing (caption Fig 35). In fresh or strong winds gybing is a tricky business and it is best to gybe when the boat is sailing fast because the apparent wind is then less strong, but it may be safer to tack instead even though it takes extra time to luff up, go about and then bear away again.

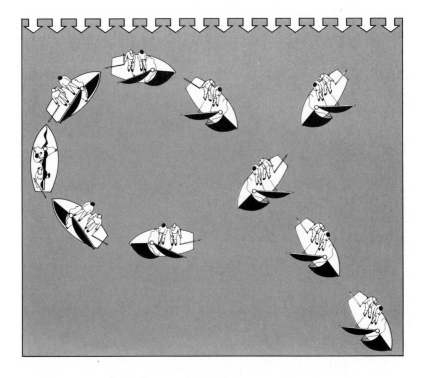

FIGURE 36: TACKING INSTEAD OF GYBING

Gybing may be considered too risky in a strong wind, and the boat can be sailed round in a full circle and tacked instead.

FIGURE 37: RETURNING TO A BEACH – ONSHORE WIND

1–3. While still seaward of the zone of breaking surf, luff head to wind and lower the mainsail.
4. Back the jib and put the tiller over so that the rudder points shoreward. 5. Run in under the jib, 6. Let the jib sheet fly, raise the centreboard and rudder blade and jump overboard, stopping her manually if she is moving too fast. In heavy surf turn her bows seaward to prevent her from being knocked sideways and overturned.

Carrying way

The helmsman has to estimate how far a boat will shoot up towards the wind before losing all way and coming to a stop, say at a pier or at a mooring buoy which is to be picked up. He luffs head to wind, the sails shake, and the boat's way through the water, her momentum, carries her forward. The distance that a boat shoots varies with her type, with conditions and with the helmsman. A heavy displacement boat carries her way farther than a lighter boat; all boats shoot farther when the wind is light and the water calm. Putting the helm hard down with a jerk brakes a boat's speed, and

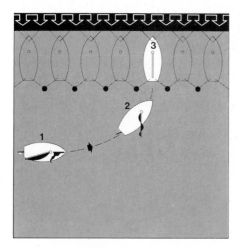

FIGURE 38: RETURNING TO A PIER – OFFSHORE WIND

1. Approach close-hauled or on a beam reach. 2. Shoot up and into the berth, lowering the jib just before turning head to wind to give the crew room on the foredeck to deal with the mooring ropes. 3. The boat shoots up to the pier to which the bow ropes are made fast, and should have lost all way when about a foot from the shore. She can be slowed if necessary by taking a turn round the posts with the mooring lines, and if she loses way before reaching the pier she can be manhandled forward.

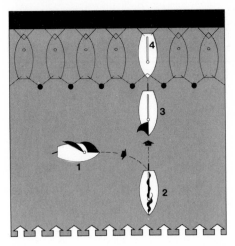

FIGURE 39: RETURNING TO A PIER OR PONTOON – ONSHORE WIND

1. Turn the boat head to wind immediately to windward of her berth. 2. Either lower the mainsail and back the jib, or back mainsail and jib so that she sails stern first into the berth. Should there be no mooring posts drop the anchor when she is head to wind at 2. and veer cable until the stern rope can be taken ashore.

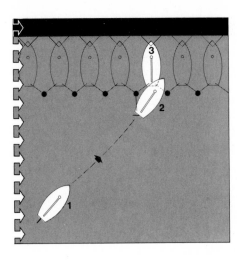

FIGURE 40: RETURNING UNDER ENGINE, WIND PARALLEL TO THE SHORE

1. Approach at an angle of about 45° and take a turn round the windward post with one bow rope and one stern rope. 2. Turn the rudder to point towards the shore and motor slow ahead to round the post and enter the berth. 3. Pass the second stern rope around the leeward post, put the helm amidships, stop the engine. A boat can rarely be steered straight into a berth with a beam wind because she sags to leeward and barely answers the helm when moving very slowly.

she carries her way farther if the helmsman applies the rudder gradually.

A boat that is shooting up too fast can sometimes be slowed by holding the mainsail out against the head wind. If sails are kept backed in this way the boat soon starts to sail stern first, and when making sternway the rudder has to be turned the opposite way to steer: making headway, tiller to starboard, rudder blade to port, turns the bows to port: making sternway, tiller to starboard turns the bows to starboard and the stern to port.

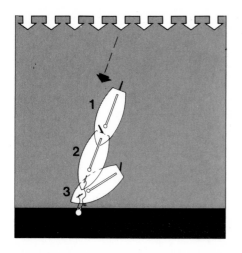

FIGURE 41: RETURNING UNDER ENGINE – ONSHORE WIND

1. Approach at an angle of about 70° and slow down by motoring full astern. Provide a good fender at the bow, stop when 1–2 feet from the pier and take the bow rope ashore. 2. Put the helm over to turn the rudder away from the pier and motor half speed astern or full speed astern if the wind is strong. 3. The wind blows the stern down and the speed at which she swings in can be controlled by regulating engine speed and altering helm angle.

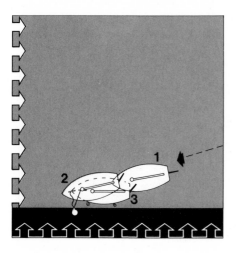

FIGURE 42: UNDER ENGINE, WIND SOMEWHERE BETWEEN OFFSHORE AND PARALLEL TO THE SHORE

1. Approach the pier slowly at an angle of about 10°, the last few yards in neutral. When 1–2 feet away from the pier stop her by motoring full astern and take the bow rope ashore. 2. Turn the rudder to point offshore and motor slow astern. Given a right-handed propeller, wheel effect helps her stern in to the pier. 3. Make fast aft and check that the fenders are correctly positioned.

Returning to the beach, a berth or a mooring

Eventually the time comes to return home and, although larger keelboats almost always return to their berths under power, especially in a congested harbour or a marina, every sailor should be able to berth under sail. The skipper makes his plans well in advance, and explains them to the crew so that they can prepare mooring ropes and put fenders out on the correct side where they will protect the topsides.

The principle is much the same, whether the boat is a light centreboarder or a heavy keelboat; the vital difference is that a heavy boat carries her way much farther and will crash into a pier if she is moving too fast, whereas a light dinghy can be stopped by hand.

Figures 38 to 42 show how to get into an awkward boxed-in berth and alongside a pier in various conditions, but picking up a mooring is usually rather easier. If boats nearby are wind-rode (head to wind) the helmsman shoots up into the wind with sails shaking and the mooring is picked up when the boat has lost all, or virtually all way. He can always sail away and try again if he has underestimated or overestimated how far she will shoot. If the boats on neighbouring moorings are tide-rode (head to tidal stream), and are lying with the wind abaft the beam, the mainsail can be lowered some way from the mooring which is approached under headsail alone, boat speed being regulated with the sheet. The mainsail can only be lowered when it is empty of wind, and the boat therefore either has to be luffed head to wind, or nearly head to wind with the mainsheet eased out at some point in the manoeuvre.

If the boat is under power, wheel effect can be very useful when coming alongside. When a propeller rotates it not only thrusts the boat forward but pushes her stern slightly to one side, acting like a wheel that is touching the sea-bed. A right-handed propeller that turns clockwise when viewed from astern pushes the stern to starboard, whereas a left-handed propeller pushes it to port. In astern gear the propeller, rotating in the reverse direction, pushes the stern the opposite way, and wheel effect is more apparent in astern gear. Most propellers are right-handed and help to tuck the stern in to starboard when in forward gear or to port when motoring astern.

Another point to remember when coming alongside under engine is that a sailing boat's reverse gear is relatively ineffective, and will not easily bring a boat to a halt, especially if there is a following wind. Furthermore, most sailing boats are more difficult to manoeuvre when motoring astern, and one with an outboard may be uncontrollable. Good judgement is essential because the boat must not be moving too fast and yet must never lose steerage way; in other words she must be moving fast enough to answer the helm but not much faster.

Lowering and furling sails, stowing etc
The crew of a keelboat prepares to lower the mainsail by topping up the boom and laying the coiled halyard on the deck the right way up so that it will run freely. The halyard is then uncleated and the sail gathered as it drops. A mainsail may be unbent and stowed in a sail bag, but it is often furled and lashed firmly to the boom with sail

tiers so that it will not blow about. A sail cover is usually laced over it for protection. The boom is lowered to rest in a notch in the crutch while the boat is moored (the crutch is removed and stowed when the boat is sailing) and the mainsheet is hauled tight, cleated and coiled. The tiller is usually lashed centrally.

The headsail is lowered and may be lashed temporarily to the guardrail or pulpit but is unhanked and bagged for longer periods. Ensign and burgee are lowered and the halyards are lashed away from the mast so that they will not slat noisily against it in the wind. Mooring ropes or anchor cable are checked to ensure that they will not chafe, fenders are sited carefully to give maximum protection, and everything is stowed in its appointed place before leaving.

A dinghy crew removes the sails and bags them, unreeves the sheets, takes out the centreboard and unships the rudder. If she is left in a dinghy park the owner may take all movable gear home for safety, and usually laces a boat cover over boom and cockpit to keep out rainwater. The boat may also have to be unrigged and the mast unstepped and stowed.

More sailing

Balance

If the boat bears away when the helmsman is holding the rudder dead amidships she is said to have lee helm because the tiller has to be held permanently to leeward to keep her on a straight course. If the boat luffs up she is said to have weather helm, and the helm is pulled to weather to correct this tendency. A boat that is well-balanced can be kept on a straight course without effort. Slight weather helm is preferred by most helmsmen because some pressure can be felt on the tiller, but excessive weather helm is tiring. A great deal of strength is then required to keep the boat on course and the rudder blade, deflected permanently to leeward at a considerable angle, acts as a brake and slows her. Pushing the helm to leeward continuously is tiring too, but lee helm is also undesirable because if the helmsman drops the tiller or falls overboard, a boat with weather helm will luff up head to wind and stop whereas one with lee helm will bear away and may accelerate, gybe or capsize.

Balance is partly a question of design and is governed by the relative positions of the centre of effort (CE) and the centre of lateral

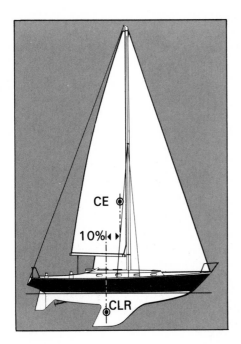

FIGURE 43 : BALANCE

The total pressure of the wind on every part of all the sails can be imagined as acting at a single point which is called the centre of effort, CE; similarly all the forces that resist sideways movement through the water act at the centre of lateral resistance, CLR. A keelboat is normally considered to be well-balanced when her CE lies about 10% of her waterline length ahead of her CLR. Neither the CE nor the CLR are static; for example, the CLR shifts when the boat heels. When the CLR moves further forward weather helm increases and the boat tries to luff up, but when the CE moves further forward the boat carries lee helm and the tiller has to be pushed to leeward to keep her on course.

resistance (CLR). Just as a body can be balanced on a pinpoint at its centre of gravity because the weight of its particles in any one direction is balanced by the weight of those in the opposite direction, so can the total force of the wind blowing on every particle of every sail that is set be imagined as acting at a pinpoint, the centre of effort.

Similarly the CLR is the point in the lateral plane through which the forces that resist sideways movement can be said to act. When the CE is too far forward of the CLR, wind pressure on the sails forces the bow to leeward and the boat suffers from lee helm. This can be corrected by shifting the CLR further forward or the CE further aft, for example by:

Setting the traveller as far to windward as possible
Reducing the headsail area
Stepping the mast nearer the stern, or raking it further aft
Increasing the mainsail area, perhaps by shaking out a reef
Lowering a pivoting centreboard
Shifting weight forward

Excessive weather helm is reduced by shifting the CE further forward or the CLR further aft, for example by:

Setting the traveller as far to leeward as possible
Increasing the headsail area
Raking the mast further forward, or stepping it nearer the bow
Reducing the area of the mainsail, generally by tucking or rolling in a reef
Raising a pivoting centreboard
Shifting weight aft

How fast does a boat sail?

As can be seen in Figure 24 a boat sails relatively slowly when she is hard on the wind; she also sails slowly when she is running because the apparent wind is least strong on that point of sailing. Her fastest course is at an angle of about 90° to the wind.

Hull speed, or displacement speed, is the maximum speed that can be made by a displacement boat − as opposed to a planing boat. When she thrusts her way through the water she raises bow and stern waves and, at hull speed, the length of the wave she raises matches her waterline length. She is supported by waves at bow and stern, and settles in the trough between them. Setting extra sails or opening the engine throttle to try to increase speed only increases the size of the bow and stern waves, and the boat is unable to escape from the wave system she herself has created. Maximum speed is therefore governed by waterline length, (L) and hull speed (V) in knots can be calculated from the equation:

$$V = \sqrt{L} \times 1{\cdot}34 \text{ (length in feet)} \quad V = \sqrt{L} \times 2{\cdot}43 \text{ (length in metres)}$$

Thus a keelboat, waterline length 29 ft (8·84 m), has a hull speed of 7·22 knots. The theoretical hull speed of a boat may sometimes be exceeded when she surfs on the crest of a breaking wave but, on the other hand, an undercanvassed (too little sail area) heavy displacement cruiser may be unable to sail at her hull speed. The formula is not valid for planing boats whose maximum speed can only be found from experience.

Planing

A dinghy with adequate sail area and a lightweight hull designed for planing can escape from her wave system. At a speed-to-length ratio of about 1·36 ($V/\sqrt{L} = 1{\cdot}36$) she climbs on to her own bow wave which shifts further aft; wetted area is reduced, together with frictional resistance, and she accelerates to plane at a speed exceeding hull speed, supported partly by buoyancy and partly by dynamic lift.

Most modern dinghies plane, as do catamarans, trimarans and some light displacement keelboats. At the critical moment the helmsman feels pressure on the rudder ease, crew weight is shifted aft to offload the bows and, frequently, hardening in the mainsheet sharply is enough to start her planing.

Sitting out and trapezing

Sailing dinghies are designed to sail on an even keel, so sail slower when heeling; helmsman and crew therefore shift their weight to windward to counter the pressure of the wind on the sails. A few boats have a sliding seat which is pushed out on the windward side so that the crew can sit well outboard while manning the jib sheet, but sitting out is more usual. Crew and helmsman sit on the side deck with their feet hooked under toe straps fitted fore-and-aft in the cockpit, and the harder that the wind blows the farther they lean back to windward. Keelboats should not be allowed to heel excessively either, and the crew of a racing boat can often be seen lined up on the weather gunwale, facing outboard with their feet dangling over the topsides.

Many dinghy classes have a trapeze on which the crew hangs, standing right out to windward with his feet braced against the

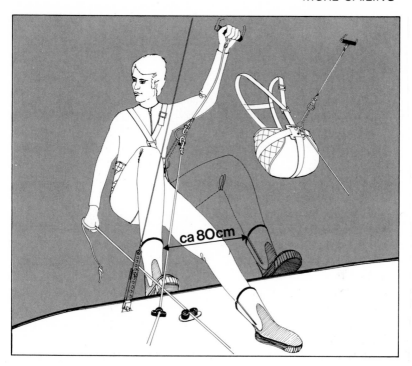

FIGURE 44: TRAPEZE WORK

The crew wears a trapeze belt or harness which distributes the load over his back and hips when he is hooked on to the trapeze wire. Thrusting his forward leg against the shroud he leans backwards, hanging all his weight on the wire. He shifts his after leg to the side deck and, holding the jib sheet in his forward hand, pushes himself outboard with the other hand and straightens his legs. His feet are about 30 in apart. As he shifts his weight outboard his body swings in an arc round his forward foot, which is braced against the shroud to counter the forward pull from the trapeze wire. The sequence is reversed when coming inboard.

gunwale. He can keep the boat virtually level, even in fresher breezes, and can continue to sail in winds that would be too strong for a boat without a trapeze, but he must react extremely quickly to every change in wind speed or alteration of course. First class co-ordination between helmsman and crew is essential, and the helmsman must give sufficient warning, say if he intends to go about, because the crew has to get back into the cockpit and transfer his weight to the opposite side at the right moment.

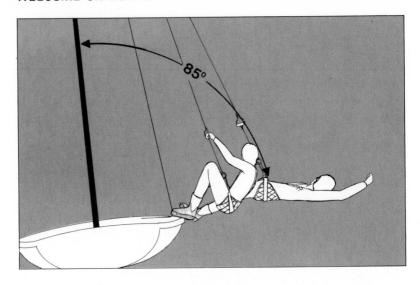

FIGURE 45: THE CORRECT TRAPEZE POSITION

The length of the trapeze wire is such that, when the crew stands out, his body lies at an angle of about 85° to the mast. When the wind eases temporarily he bends both knees to bringing his weight inboard and prevent the boat from heeling to windward. An experienced crew can come inboard by bending his knees, raising his feet above the side deck and swinging in on the wire.

FIGURE 46: THE SPINNAKER

The spinnaker is prepared for hoisting by attaching the halyard to the head and the sheets to the two clews. The sheets lead outside the forestay and shrouds, and are rove through blocks or fairleads aft; the sheet to windward is called the guy and controls the tack. The spinnaker pole is clipped to the guy to extend the sail to windward, and is connected at the mast to a fitting that is often mounted on a track so that the pole can be raised or lowered to a horizontal position; the downhaul and topping lift prevent the pole from lifting and dropping respectively. When the sail has been hoisted the guy and sheet are hardened to fill the spinnaker. On a run the guy hauls the spinnaker pole back to the shrouds and the sheet is eased well out, but when beam reaching the spinnaker is set shy with the pole almost touching the forestay and the sheet well hardened in. Spinnaker trimming calls for concentration; when the luff trembles the sheet needs to be hardened slightly, but if the luff falls in either the guy has to be eased and the sheet hardened or the helmsman has to bear away slightly. If the pole is too far forward the centre of the sail collapses; either the guy needs to be hardened and the sheet eased, or the helmsman luffs up to fill the sail.

Sailing with a spinnaker

A spinnaker is made of light and often brightly-coloured sailcloth, and is cut very full. Its area may well be greater than that of mainsail and headsail combined, and it is most often set in light and moderate winds when broad reaching and running. Spinnaker design has become highly specialised, especially in the offshore racing field, and sailmakers have developed different cuts for all weathers and various courses, for example the flatter star-cut spinnaker which can be set even on a close reach.

When the spinnaker is hoisted on a run, the headsail is virtually useless and may even be harmful and it is therefore normally

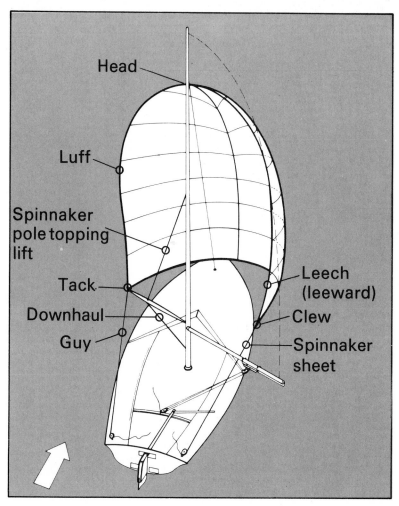

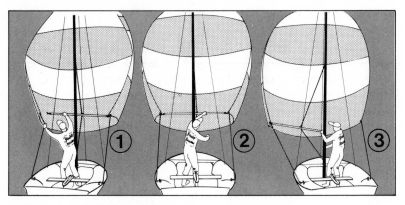

FIGURE 47 : GYBING THE SPINNAKER

Spinnaker and mainsail are gybed simultaneously. The method illustrated is only suitable if the foredeck hand is strong enough to control the spinnaker when it is full of wind. 1. Detach the spinnaker pole from the mast and clip it to what was the sheet but is about to become the guy. 2. Unclip the pole from what was the guy. 3. Attach it to the mast fitting and adjust guy and sheet. The topping lift takes the weight of the pole while it is being moved from one side to the other.

Larger boats often carry two spinnaker poles and the sail is then always connected to the mast by one pole. Another alternative is to unclip the spinnaker pole from the guy and to slack off the topping lift so that the pole can be dipped beneath the forestay and clipped to the new guy on the other side.

lowered. In lighter breezes an offshore racer may set a big boy to balance the spinnaker, and the mainsail may then be reefed to reduce its blanketing effect. The headsail may still draw effectively on a reach, but may be replaced by a spinnaker staysail if the keelboat has a comprehensive wardrobe of sails.

The caption to Fig 46 explains how to hoist a spinnaker, but it is not easy to control such a large sail, set flying (attached only at the three corners, whereas mainsail and headsail are attached to mast and stay respectively by their luffs). The crew of a keelboat may use a turtle, a bag into which the spinnaker is packed carefully, with halyard and sheets attached to head and clews. The turtle is secured to the foredeck or pulpit and the spinnaker, which is hoisted directly out of it, should set without twisting. Another alternative is to hoist the sail in stops, that is, with light cotton lashed around it at intervals; hardening the sheet breaks the cotton and allows the spinnaker to fill with wind. Many dinghies have a spinnaker chute, which is a tubular container that leads aft from a funnel-like opening in the foredeck. The spinnaker lies in it ready to be hoisted, with halyard and sheets attached. When the spinnaker is lowered, a line, sewn to the centre of the sail, pulls it down into the chute ready to be rehoisted.

A spinnaker cannot be lowered when it is full of wind, and in smaller boats guy and sheet may be slacked off until the sail collapses. In larger keelboats the guy is usually unshackled from the tack and the sail flies out to leeward like a flag. It is then lowered in the lee of the mainsail and is gathered on the side deck or pulled beneath the boom and into the cockpit. The pole can then be stowed.

Trim, tuning and controls

Sails are trimmed by adjusting their angle to the centreline with the sheets, but the word trim also refers to the way a boat floats. Normally she should float on an even keel, parallel to her designed waterline, but she will be trimmed by the stern and float with her bows tilted up if, say, too much heavy gear is stowed in the afterpeak. No boat performs well when incorrectly trimmed, and dinghies are particularly sensitive. The crew of a dinghy sit fairly far forward when close-hauled to prevent the transom from dragging through the water, but shift their weight further aft when reaching to encourage her to plane. In very light airs they may trim her by the head deliberately to raise the afterbody clear of the water and reduce wetted area and friction.

Tuning, rather like tuning a musical instrument to perfection, is a question of adjusting the rigging so that the sails will produce their best performance, or maximum drive when they are set on the mast and spars. A sail is an aerofoil, and the amount of lift produced by the sail depends on its camber or fullness, that is, on how much it curves. Camber is adjusted to match the point of sailing and the strength of the wind and, briefly, a fuller sail is more powerful and suitable for light winds and when reaching or running, but the boat will heel less with a flatter sail in stronger winds and when close-hauled. Mainsail camber can be varied by adjusting the standing rigging to bend the mast, by altering the tension of the foot with the outhaul and that of the luff with the downhaul or a Cunningham hole (Fig 5), by adjusting the position of the mainsheet traveller (Figs 11 7, 13 33) etc. The camber of a headsail can also be controlled by varying luff tension and the sheet lead, and headsail sheets are often rove through a sliding fairlead or block which can be shifted to the desired position along a track bolted to the deck either fore-and-aft or at an angle to the centreline. The fairleads of many high-performance boats can be adjusted both fore-and-aft and athwartships. (Figs 13 19).

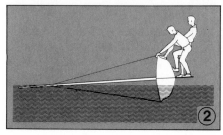

FIGURE 48: RIGHTING A CAPSIZED DINGHY

1. Turn the bow towards the wind; if the mast were to point to windward the wind, getting under the sail, would whip mast and sail right over and capsize the boat on the other side. One man holds her by the bow and swims towards the wind, which helps to push her stern round. Mainsheet and jib sheet must be uncleated before attempting to right the boat; if they do not run free the wind will fill the sails and capsize her again.

2. One man standing on the centreboard can lever a boat upright, but his weight pushes her down and, unless she has generous side buoyancy tanks, the cockpit will be full when she has been righted.

Capsizing and righting a dinghy

All centreboard dinghies can be capsized, and must carry enough buoyancy to enable them to float when full of water with the crew on board. Each member of the crew wears a buoyancy aid or life-jacket to keep him afloat, even if he is a strong swimmer, because he could be knocked half senseless or even unconscious if struck on the head by the boom.

The most important rule is – never leave the boat – not even if a paddle or the rudder is floating only a few strokes away. A fresh wind will make a capsized boat drift downwind much faster than a person can swim.

A boat is most likely to capsize in gusty weather, but if the helmsman keeps a good lookout he is warned of an approaching gust when he sees a patch of darker, rippled water. When the gust strikes he spills wind by easing out the mainsheet far enough to prevent the boat from heeling violently and, as soon as the gust has passed, hardens the mainsheet again so that the boat can gather full way and become more stable. If a gust strikes a dinghy when she is

64

3 Less water accumulates if the crew swim round and raise the mast by hand. One person must keep hold of a rope attached to the boat to prevent her from drifting away because it is rarely possible to swim fast enough to catch up with her.

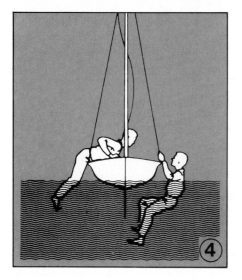

4. One of the crew hauls himself aboard while the other steadies the boat from the other side. When sailing single-handed it is often easier to scramble over the stern. If the cockpit is full, some water has to be bailed out manually before opening the self-bailer and sailing the dinghy dry on a fast reach.

making very little or no way she is virtually helpless and will capsize instantly.

A light racing dinghy capsizes relatively easily but can be righted extremely quickly by an experienced crew, and more slowly by beginners, as shown in Fig 45.

Although a heavy dinghy is much more stable and does not capsize so readily she is very much more difficult to right and the crew may fail to get her back on an even keel. They then sit on the gunwale, or on the bottom if she has turned turtle, and wait for help. The internationally recognised distress signal is to raise and lower both arms slowly and repeatedly to either side. Under no circumstances should the crew leave the boat; it has been proved all too often that people underestimate the distance to the shore and overestimate their own strength, particularly when the sea is rough and the water cold. It is also much easier to spot a person on a drifting boat than a head in the water.

If a boat offers to take the dinghy in tow, lower and lash the sails and check that no clothing or ropes which could foul the propeller are dragging in the water. Take a turn round the mast with the tow rope, but do not knot it in case you want to cast off in a hurry. When under tow raise the centreboard to prevent the boat from sheering off to one side, keep crew weight aft to stop the bows burying and stay dead astern of the towing boat.

Heaving to

When heaving to, the helmsman puts the boat about normally, but the crew does not uncleat the jib sheet; she lies with the wind slightly forward of the beam and the jib aback, making no headway but considerable leeway. Usually the tiller is lashed or held to leeward, and the mainsail may need to be eased slightly. A boat may heave to for many reasons, such as when waiting for the tidal stream to turn or, because she sails comparatively quietly when hove to, to ease her motion while repairs are made or a meal is cooked. Many sailors heave to in bad weather, but boats with long keels behave better in these conditions than modern boats with short keels.

Reefing and heavy weather

When the wind freshens markedly, sail area has to be reduced for a number of reasons, other than the obvious fact that too much canvas overloads the gear and may, for example, cause the standing rigging to part and the boat to be dismasted. A keelboat sails more slowly when she heels excessively; not only does she then make more leeway, which is undesirable, but the helmsman often finds it difficult to keep her under control because of increased weather helm. An overcanvassed dinghy reaches the point where the helmsman cannot keep her on course because he constantly has either to luff up or to ease the mainsheet to spill wind and prevent her from capsizing.

The crew of a keelboat can shorten sail by replacing the large genoa with a jib, or by changing down from a larger jib to a smaller; they can also take in the mainsail of a ketch or yawl. Some boats have a roller jib, and this can be furled to whatever extent is desirable by rolling the luff round the luff spar. A few boats carry furling gear for the mainsail as well, but in most boats the area of the main is reduced by roller, points or jiffy reefing, as in Fig 49.

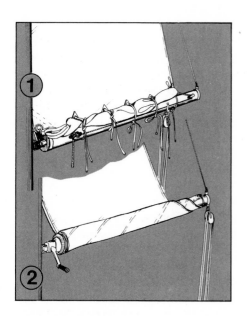

FIGURE 49: REEFING

1. Points reefing. The topping lift is tightened to take the weight of the boom and sail, and the halyard is eased until the reef points are level with the boom. The luff cringle is pulled down and lashed to the boom at the gooseneck. The leech pendant, with which the leech cringle is brought down, runs up from one side of the boom, through the cringle, down through a cheek block on the other side of the boom and is cleated forward. The reef points are tied either beneath a boom that is grooved to take the foot, or beneath the foot of a sail that has slides. The luff is then tensioned with the halyard winch, or the halyard is swigged up manually, and the topping lift is slacked off. The entire load is taken by the pendants, while the reef points keep the bunt of the sail furled. Jiffy reefing is similar but quicker, the cringle at the luff being slipped over a hook on the boom; larger boats have a winch on the boom to help the crew to pull down the leech cringle.

2. Roller reefing. The foot is rolled round the boom, usually with a worm gear operated by turning a handle, but sometimes with a ratchet and pawl. With a through-mast system the reefing handle is generally forward of the mast. Most boats with roller reefing have a stern mainsheet system and no kicking strap, as in the figure. When roller reefing a boat with a centre mainsheet (see Fig 13), the mainsheet block is attached to a reefing claw and the kicking strap has a long strap attached; this is rolled in between the layers of sail.

   Roller reefing is preferred sometimes because a weaker crew can shorten sail more speedily and because the amount of sail taken in can be varied infinitely instead of being limited to one, two or three big reefs. On the other hand, with points reefing the boom does not sag and the sail sets better. Many racing keelboat crews consider jiffy reefing the fastest and most effective method, and many racing dinghy classes never reef at all.

A dinghy's mainsail is normally reefed by pulling the boom aft to disconnect it from the gooseneck, rolling the sail round it as often as necessary, and pushing the boom back on to the gooseneck again. Many dinghies, especially those with a trapeze, cannot be reefed at all, and when the wind is so strong that the crew cannot keep the boat upright, sailing has to be abandoned for the day. If the crew of a dinghy sailing inland are surprised by a sudden squall, they can lower the jib and sail back to the shore under mainsail alone, or lower the mainsail and reach or run back with only the jib set.

A keelboat that sails far offshore may be caught out in a gale, and there are a number of different ways in which she can ride out the storm. The method adopted will depend on whether there are any dangers nearby, the direction of the wind, the size and steepness of the seas and the design of the boat. Some boats lie a-hull comfortably, roughly broadside on to the seas, others may heave to, or run before the storm, often under bare poles with no sails set. In some boats and conditions it may be best to run downwind fast, but excessive speed may cause another boat to be pooped by following seas which break over the stern; a long warp may then be streamed astern to slow her and keep her stern on to the seas. She may also lie comfortably to a sea anchor (a tapering conical bag, open at both ends), streamed to keep her at a certain angle to the waves. It is essential to avoid being caught in a gale without ample searoom to leeward. Clawing off a lee shore is extremely difficult because the boat has to beat to windward under minimal canvas, making a great deal of leeway, and the seas become steeper and more dangerous as the water shoals.

Man overboard

It is relatively rare for the crew of a dinghy to fall overboard, and if he does he is often still holding on to the mainsheet or jib sheet. A dinghy loses way so quickly that the man in the water, wearing his buoyancy aid, often has no more than a few strokes to swim to her when she stops, either as a result of luffing head to wind, or when the jib and mainsheet are let fly. In any case a dinghy is so handy that the crew left on board should have no difficulty in sailing back to pick up his mate from the water, say after lowering the spinnaker.

So far as keelboats are concerned, prevention is better than cure, and non-slip decks, together with the pulpits at bow and stern and the guardrail round the sides, considerably reduce the risk of falling overboard. Some larger boats have solid bulwarks in place of a

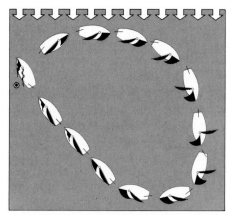

FIGURE 50: MAN OVERBOARD – CLOSE-HAULED OR REACHING

Throw a lifebuoy towards the man and keep an eye on his position in the water. The quickest method of returning is to bear away, gybe and sail back close-hauled. If the wind is very strong and gybing too risky, go about instead.

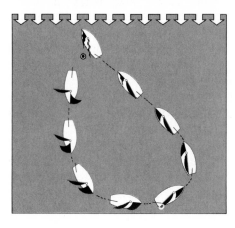

FIGURE 51: MAN OVERBOARD – RUNNING

Throw a lifebuoy towards the man and keep an eye on him. Luff up, tack and sail back to him close-hauled. If a spinnaker is set it must be lowered before luffing up.

guardrail. The crew must take care and should wear safety harnesses which have webbing straps fitting over the shoulders and round the chest, with a lifeline attached centrally on the chest. One hand for yourself and one for the boat is an old adage, but frequently the crew needs both hands for the boat, say when changing headsails on the foredeck or when reefing the mainsail while the boat is pitching or rolling violently. He therefore snaps himself on to a solid part of the boat with one of the two hooks on his safety harness lifeline and will still be connected to the boat should he lose his footing and fall in. If this should happen, the helmsman must take all way off the boat immediately so that the crew is not pulled underwater by her speed. It is only good sense to wear life-jackets in heavy weather: many people are reluctant to put them on because they are bulky, but inconvenience is always preferable to drowning!

69

Even after taking precautions people can fall overboard, and a keelboat must be equipped for such emergencies. A horseshoe lifebuoy is stowed close by the helmsman, ready to be thrown to a person in the water. Attached to the lifebuoy by a line is a water light which operates automatically when it turns to float right way up. A boat taking part in a long-distance race offshore is required to carry a lifebuoy with a dan buoy that has a flag on top of an 8 ft (2·5m) pole, as well as a dye marker to colour the water and mark the man's position for searching aircraft or vessels.

When someone is seen to fall in the crew is warned by the shout, 'Man overboard', the lifebuoy is immediately thrown towards the person in the water and, because it is all too easy to lose sight of a head in breaking seas, one of the crew is detailed to keep his eyes on him, regardless of alterations of course.

Obviously the quicker that the person is recovered the better; it is demoralizing to see one's boat sailing away, perhaps hidden from sight at times by the waves. A boat with a reliable engine and adequate crew can turn head to wind and motor back to the person once the sails have been lowered. Mainsail and headsail need not be lowered if the person fell in when the boat was on a run, and she can return under power with sails shaking. On the other hand, if the boat has no engine, or has insufficient crew to lower sails, start the engine and keep an eye on the man in the water, go about or gybe and sail back to him. If the boat is close-hauled or reaching, the helmsman bears away, gybes, and returns close-hauled, but if she is on a run he luffs up until the boat is hard on the wind and then tacks. Gybing and tacking will probably take longer than usual with the crew one member short.

When approaching someone in the water, the boat should not shoot up to him head to wind as if he were a mooring buoy about to be picked up. One method is to approach slowly from leeward, luffing gently at the right moment so that contact can be made and a lifeline passed round him when he is just abaft the beam. Good judgement is needed because the bow wave will wash him out of reach if the boat is sailing too fast, but she will lose steerage way if she is too slow. Alternatively, the helmsman approaches a little to windward of him, the crew let the sheets fly and the boat is allowed to drift down quietly towards him.

Getting someone back on board presents problems, and anybody who has swum from a boat with topsides over 2 ft 6 in (80 cms) high will realise that a ladder is needed, with rungs that extend below the waterline. The problem is aggravated by the guardrail, and if the lower lifeline is so close to the deck that a crew wearing a bulky lifejacket cannot be hauled on board beneath it a gangway should be provided between two stanchions or as in Fig 14 31. A conscious crew wearing safety harness can be helped through the gangway by hauling on the webbing, or on large diameter rope passed under his arms and under each thigh. An unconcious crew or one weakened by cold and unable to help himself, is even more diffcult to recover, but it may be possible to raise him from the water with the aid of the boom and topping lift or a halyard, or to roll him back on board with the help of the seas and by hauling on two ropes, made fast in the cockpit and passed beneath his body and back on board.

Running aground

A boat should always keep well clear of dangers such as rocks, wrecks or submerged structures which could damage hull or rudder, but running aground where the bottom is soft is not always a sign of incompetence, and is generally inconvenient rather than dangerous. Keelboats and centreboard dinghies alike often risk running aground on mud or sand by sailing really close to the shore, to avoid a river current or the waters where a foul (adverse) tidal stream runs fastest. When cheating the tide in this way, the crew of a smaller keelboat measures the depth of the water with a sounding pole, while keelboats that draw more water carry an echo sounder, or one of the crew sounds with a lead attached to a marked line.

A dinghy that has run aground on a windward shore will sail off again as soon as the crew raises the centreboard, but it is much more difficult to get off a lee shore, and the wind just pushes a dinghy into still shallower water if her centreboard is raised. The crew can only jump overboard to push her clear if the bottom is hard. If she grounds on soft mud, and the crew fail to push her off with paddle and jib-stick or spinnaker pole, the sails have to be lowered and the boat paddled or rowed some way offshore where the sails can be rehoisted.

In tidal waters a keelboat that runs aground on a rising tide will soon refloat, but if the tide is falling she may have to wait several hours and may perhaps be left high and dry at low water, with the sea-bed visible all around.

When a keelboat runs aground on a windward shore the crew can try to get her free by increasing her angle of heel to reduce her draft slightly, and they shift their weight to leeward and harden in the mainsheet fully. A boat can also sometimes be freed immediately by motoring full astern, and if the bottom is soft it may help if the crew rock her by running from side to side to enlarge the groove she made when grounding. If a keelboat is stuck hard and fast on a lee shore the sails are handed (lowered) and the boat may be kedged off; the kedge (a light anchor) is then run out in the dinghy to be dropped some distance to windward and, when the boat refloats she is hauled out to lie to the kedge while sails are rehoisted.

The worst time to run aground is at high water springs, and every effort must be made to refloat the boat at the following high water. Lightening her by taking off all movable gear reduces her draft, and another boat with a powerful engine may then be able to tow her off. If even this attempt fails, she will be beneaped and will not refloat before the next spring tides a fortnight later.

Anchoring

A boat does not carry an anchor just to enable the crew to 'park' her while they go ashore or have a swim; it is a vital part of her equipment. Lives may depend on the anchor holding, for example if a dismasted or uncontrollable boat is being driven onto a danger. A boat can be anchored in sheltered bays or in harbours that have no

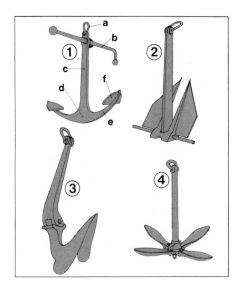

FIGURE 52: TYPES OF ANCHOR

1. Fisherman: the best all-round anchor, holds relatively well on stones and weed, and holds 7–10 times its own weight on sand. a) ring, b) folding stock secured with a pin, c) shaft, d) crown, e) arms, f) flukes.
2. Danforth: holding power is about three times that of a fisherman of the same weight, but it holds less well on rocks or weed.
3. CQR or Plough: greater holding power than most but less effective on heavy clay or thick seaweed.
4. Folding grapnel: the flukes hinge up to lie flush with the shaft. Lightweight, for dinghies.

trots, piles or mooring buoys for visiting boats, and in some harbours a boat lies to an anchor with her stern moored to a pier while in others she is moored bows on to the shore and runs out a stern anchor. A crew can slow a boat down as she approaches a berth, by dropping the anchor astern.

There are several points to consider when selecting an anchorage:
- Shelter from wind and sea. Beware of anchoring near a lee shore, or one that is likely to become a lee shore if the wind shifts as forecast. The boat will be stranded if the anchor drags.
- The sea-bed: hard sand is good holding ground; mud and clay are less good, and a slimy weed-covered bottom is poorest of all. Avoid foul ground, littered with old anchors, cables and obstructions, as well as prohibited anchorages where cables are laid on the sea-bed.
- Anchor well clear of a busy fairway, and allow swinging room so that the boat can swing full circle round her anchor without striking obstructions or running aground when the direction of the wind or tidal stream changes.
- Suitable anchorages are usually marked on charts, the symbol being an anchor.

A modern anchor design such as a CQR or Bruce need not be as heavy as the traditional fisherman type. As a rough guide, for normal cruising, the weights of anchors are as follows:

Displacement	Fisherman	Modern design
Up to 2 tons	44 lbs (20 kg)	22 lbs (10 kg)
Up to 4 tons	55 lbs (25 kg)	29 lbs (13 kg)
Up to 7 tons	66 lbs (30 kg)	33 lbs (15 kg)
Up to 10 tons	100 lbs (45 kg)	44 lbs (20 kg)

Many keelboats carry a lighter kedge in addition.

Rope cable is shackled to an anchor, rather than tied on with a fisherman's bend which reduces tensile strength by about 50% and may also come undone. The amount of anchor cable veered (let out) varies with the depth of water, the type of cable used and the weather. Dinghies use rope cable, but keelboats may carry either rope or chain, and if rope is used it is best to insert about 20 ft (6 m) of chain between anchor and rope to help the anchor to dig into the ground. Depth is established with a lead or echo sounder, and allowance must be made for the rise and fall of the tide. Less scope and, therefore, less swinging room is required with chain cable, but more cable is veered when the wind freshens because the longer the anchor cable the better will the anchor hold.

The inboard end of the cable is made fast before letting go the anchor, to avoid losing both for ever. The crew lets the anchor go when the boat has lost all way and just started to make sternway, not when she is motionless, because the cable, dropping in a heap on the anchor, can get caught on a fluke that is not embedded. After enough cable has been veered, the cable is snubbed by taking a turn round the sampson post or mooring cleat, and this helps the anchor to dig into the seabed. When the anchor cable has been made fast the crew look for two objects on shore that are in line and roughly abeam. If these remain in line the anchor is holding, but if they separate the anchor is dragging and the crew either pays out more cable or weighs anchor and lets it go elsewhere. Larger boats with heavier anchors usually have a windlass or small capstan on the foredeck to help the crew weigh anchor.

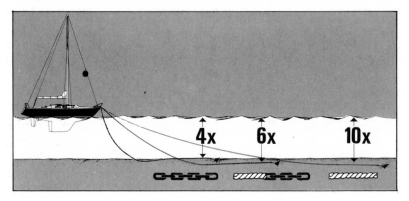

FIGURE 53: HOW MUCH CABLE SHOULD BE VEERED?

If chain cable is used the scope should be at least four times the depth of water at high water. If the cable is rope with a length of chain between the anchor and the rope, veer at least six times the depth of water, but if the cable is all rope scope should be about ten times depth. A boat at anchor exhibits a black ball by day and a white all-round light, the riding light or anchor light, by night.

Safety

Safety concerns both the crew and the boat. Collectively, the crew must be adequate in number and be sufficiently experienced for the type of sailing planned. Individually, a crew can only work safely and efficiently if he is dry, warm and able to move about freely while keeping his footing. Dinghy crews should always wear buoyancy aids to help them float after capsizing, or preferably life-jackets which turn them face upwards with mouth and nose above water, even when unconscious. In colder weather a crew often wears neoprene wet suits for warmth. The crew of a keelboat requires tough but flexible waterproof clothing, usually consisting of trousers and a jacket with a hood or separate sou'wester. Although frequently called oilskins, these are now generally made of a material coated with PVC. A safety harness and life-jacket is required for each crew member on board. Anti-seasick pills should be included in a keelboat's First Aid kit because seasickness affects efficiency and can put one or more of the crew completely out of action.

A dinghy's buoyancy is checked to ensure that she floats and will therefore act as a liferaft for the crew until help arrives, should they be unable to right her themselves and sail to safety. A keelboat may also carry buoyancy but the important points are that she is seaworthy, well-equipped and properly crewed so that she can withstand heavy weather when far offshore. Most keelboats now have watertight or self-draining cockpits from which water drains overboard instead of collecting in the bilges. The bridgedeck forward of the cockpit should be high enough to keep water out of the cabin, and the companionway washboards and all hatches should be watertight and strong enough to withstand any green seas that break heavily aboard. Pulpits, stanchions, grab rails etc., are strongly fastened to stout parts of the structure; all gear must be sound, and the anchor heavy enough to hold the boat in heavy weather. A lifebuoy with water light is stowed aft close by the helmsman, and many sailing boats carry a self-inflating liferaft large enough to accommodate the whole crew in case they have to abandon ship.

Bilge pumps must be of adequate capacity, and sited where they can be manned for long periods if necessary, and all through-hull fittings must be provided with seacocks. Fire extinguishers are positioned where they are accessible after a fire has broken out. Adequate and reliable navigation equipment is essential for seagoing boats, as well as a radio for receiving weather forecasts.

A boat must also be able to warn other vessels of her presence. At night she exhibits navigation lights (see Fig 69) and in restricted visibility the crew sounds a foghorn; these must be respectively visible and audible at a range which enables large vessels to keep clear. When a boat is near shipping lanes a radar reflector is hoisted high in the rigging so that the boat can be detected by radar-equipped vessels. Flares are also carried for emergency signals, white being ignited to draw attention to the boat's presence, red for use in case of distress. Any boat that becomes aware that another is in distress should do all she can to assist to save life, say by standing by to pick up the crew, by taking the other boat in tow, or by alerting rescue services as appropriate in the circumstances.

Racing

The cruising man has a vast range of boats from which to choose. He may enjoy pottering about in sheltered waters in a relatively stable dinghy, sailing close by the shore in a dayboat, or making short passages along the coast in a small keelboat. Then again he may prefer to test his seamanship to the full by sailing far offshore or across oceans, and his boat must then be really seaworthy and properly equipped for long ocean voyaging. There is an equally vast range of boats available for the racing man. Some boats are designed specifically for racing, speed rather than comfort being the prime consideration, others are cruiser-racers or general purpose dinghies, which are equally suitable for racing or cruising. Cost apart, his choice will depend on the time he has to spare, the number of crew available and whether he wants keen competition or just to enjoy an occasional race. Only boats which are more or less comparable can race against each other satisfactorily, and these are divided into classes as follows:

- One-design classes: the boats are all built to the same design and are virtually identical; building material, weight, hull and sail measurements being specified in the class rules. Latterly, one-design racing has spread from dinghies and small keelboats to the offshore racing field.
- Manufacturer's class boats are also one-designs, but control over their fittings and gear is so much tighter that the differences in performance between one boat and another results only from the skill of the crew.
- Development or restricted-class boats are not identical. Some measurements are controlled, such as overall length, beam or sail area, and the minimum weight is often specified. Other measurements are left open for the individual designer to develop as he sees fit, and the boats may vary greatly in appearance. These classes present a challenge to both designer and crew.
- Boats of completely different designs can race against each other in handicap classes. The time that a boat takes to complete the course, her elapsed time, is amended in accordance with a handicapping formula or system to establish her corrected time, and the winner is the boat with the shortest corrected time. Smaller handicap classes often race under the *Portsmouth Yardstick* system, which is based on the recorded past performance of boats in various

classes. The elapsed time of each boat is corrected according to the Portsmouth number allocated for her class.

● Offshore racing yachts differ widely in type and measurements: they are measured and given a rating which is calculated from the extremely complicated *International Offshore Rule*, the IOR. A larger, faster boat has a higher rating than a smaller slower boat, and the time multiplication factor, based on the rating, is applied to elapsed time to find corrected time. IOR-rated boats vary so greatly in size that the largest yachts race in conditions which are often quite different from those met by the smallest, and race organisers, such as the British *Royal Ocean Racing Club*, divide competitors into classes based on their ratings.

● In level racing classes competition is between boats with an IOR rating no higher than that specified for their class, such as 27·5 ft for the One-Ton class. Although the boats' individual measurements may vary enormously, they are not handicapped and the first boat to cross the line is the winner.

● The Metre classes, such as the Twelve Metres that compete for the America's Cup, are also built to a rule. Measurements such as displacement, sail area, beam and length vary from boat to boat and a boat with, say, greater sail area than another has to pay the penalty of greater displacement if her rating is not to exceed 12 metres.

● An international class is one that is recognised by the governing body of yacht racing, the *International Yacht Racing Union*, IYRU. The boats are well distributed in many different countries. The IYRU also selects the Olympic classes which in 1984 are the Soling, Star, Flying Dutchman, Tornado, 470, Finn and Windglider.

● National classes are raced widely within a country, and are often administered by the national authority which in the UK is the *Royal Yachting Association*, the RYA.

● Catamarans race both in one-design classes and in divisions which are based on hull measurements and sail area. The C division catamarans which compete for the International Catamaran Challenge Trophy frequently experiment with unconventional rigs and are extraordinarily fast.

Although the course round which boats race may vary in length from thousands of miles across an ocean to a mile or two round some buoys on an inland reservoir every course has a starting line and a finishing line, and there are usually a number of marks which have to be left to port or to starboard. The details of the race, the course, signals and any special regulations such as those stipulating what equipment must be carried, are printed in the sailing

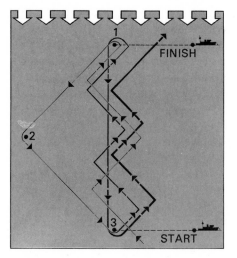

FIGURE 54: OLYMPIC COURSE

Start – beat to 1, the windward mark – broad reach to 2, the reaching mark – broad reach to 3, the lee mark – beat again to 1 – run to 3 – beat to the finish. In races other than Olympics the boats often sail two triangles and, instead of finishing as above, may sail from 1–2–3 and finish.

instructions. The starting and finishing lines may or may not be the same, and may extend between two buoys or between a committee boat and a buoy. A line may also be the extension of the line between two posts on shore. The marks to be rounded are frequently laid specially for races inland or close by the coast, but those for offshore races are generally light buoys, lighthouses or other permanent aids to navigation.

Offshore races are from one harbour to another, or around specified marks and back to the starting point, but round-the-buoys racing often involves sailing more than once around a very short course. A fair test of sailing skills is provided by a triangular course with marks so laid that the boats spend more time beating than reaching and running. There may be just one race, but major events such as championships and the Olympics are decided by a race series; a race winner is then awarded 0 points and the champion is the man who accumulates the lowest total of points over the whole series, usually after discarding the points awarded for his worst result. Offshore racing boats competing for the Admiral's Cup, the Southern Cross and the Ton Class cups compete in a series which consists of a mixture of round-the-buoys races inshore, and two offshore races.

There are also specialised forms of racing such as match racing, when one boat or one helmsman competes against only one other boat or helmsman. In team racing three boats compete as a team against three other boats, and the positions of all the boats in the team determines which is the winning team.

WELCOME ON BOARD

The race officers make three signals when starting a race. The warning signal, often the class flag, is followed five minutes later by the preparatory signal, normally code flag P; the boats have to comply with the racing rules from that moment on. The race starts at the starting signal which is made exactly ten minutes after the warning signal, and any boat on the course side of the line when the signal is made is recalled and has to start again. An audible signal is made simultaneously with each visual signal.

During the race all boats have to abide by the IYRU racing rules, which are based on the Collision Regulations, (see Rule of the Road,

FIGURE 55: BOAT CLASSES (1)

OPTIMIST   crew one child

1	LOA 2·34 m	LWL 1·75 m	Beam 1·13 m	Draft 0·77 m
	Weight 50 kg	Sail area 3·30 sq m		

OK   1 crew

2	LOA 4·00 m	LWL 3·80 m	Beam 1·42 m	Draft 0·90 m
	Weight 85 kg	Sail area 7·28 sq m		

MIRROR   2 crew

3	LOA 3·35 m	LWL 2·95 m	Beam 1·40 m	Draft 0·70 m
	Weight 60 kg	Sail area 6·5 sq m		

505   2 crew

4	LOA 5·05 m	LWL 4·57 m	Beam 1·86 m	Draft 1·13 m
	Weight 130 kg	Mainsail 11·7 sq m	Jib 4·61 sq m	

420   2 crew

5	LOA 4·20 m	LWL 4·02 m	Beam 1·63 m	Draft 0·97 m
	Weight 120 kg	Mainsail 7·45 sq m	Jib 2·80 sq m	

LASER   1 crew

6	LOA 4·23 m	LWL 3·81 m	Beam 1·37 m	Draft 0·90 m
	Weight 57 kg	Sail area 7·06 sq m		

FIGURE 56: BOAT CLASSES (2): OLYMPIC CLASSES

SOLING   3 crew

7	LOA 8·15 m	LWL 6·10 m	Beam 1·90 m	Draft 1·30 m
	Weight 1000 kg	Sail area 21·70 sq m		Olympic class since 1972

TORNADO   2 crew

8	LOA 6·10 m	LWL 5·58 m	Beam 3·05 m	Draft 0·76 m
	Weight 135 kg	Sail area 21·8 sq m		Olympic class since 1976

STAR   2 crew

9	LOA 6·90 m	LWL 4·72 m	Beam 1·73 m	Draft 1·01 m
	Weight 900 kg	Mainsail 20·15 sq m	Jib 5·85 sq m	First selected as an Olympic class in 1932

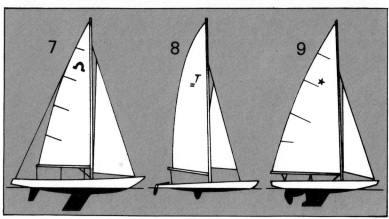

page 38) in that port tack boat gives way to starboard tack, and windward boat gives way to leeward boat. The rules must be studied carefully before taking part in a race because they specify which boat has right of way in every situation that can arise when boats compete in extremely close company. For example, they specify when a boat may call for water to avoid running aground or hitting an obstruction, when she may luff an opponent that is overtaking to windward, and when the outside boat is required to allow room to

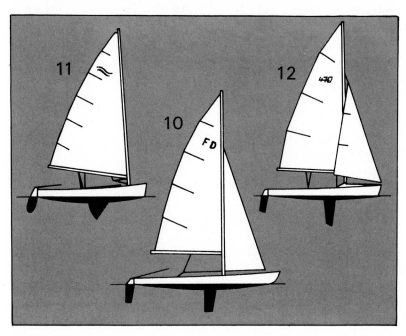

FIGURE 57: BOAT CLASSES (3): OLYMPIC CLASSES

FLYING DUTCHMAN   2 crew

10 LOA 6·05 m	LWL 5·50 m	Beam 1·80 m	Draft 1·10 m
Weight 130 kg	Mainsail 10 sq m	Headsail 5·00 sq m	Olympic class since 1960

FINN   1 crew

11 LOA 4·50 m	LWL 4·05 m	Beam 1·51 m	Draft 0·85 m
Weight 105 kg	Sail area 10 sq m		Olympic class since 1952

470   2 crew

12 LOA 4·70 m	LWL 4·44 m	Beam 1·68 m	Draft 1·05 m
Weight 115 kg	Mainsail 9·70 sq m	Jib 3·58 sq m	Olympic class since 1976.

an inside boat so that she can round the mark. A boat can protest against another that breaks a rule and, unless that boat retires or performs an alternative penalty when this is allowed, she will be disqualified by the race committee who hear the protest after the race.

Many factors contribute towards winning races: boat speed is clearly important and calls for careful tuning of the rig, efficient gear and controls, good helming and crewing etc., as well as a smooth and weed-free bottom, but a boat that is sailing faster may not reach the mark as quickly as a slower one whose helmsman's tactics are better: he may have noticed a wind shift and taken advantage of it, or made better use of the tidal stream, and will have learnt the rules so thoroughly that he can use them to good advantage without breaking them.

Sailors who are not competitively minded benefit from an occasional race; beginners learn more quickly and the sailing skills of the more experienced are sharpened.

Navigation

Charts

The chart that the sailor uses to find out where he can sail safely is not unlike a road map, and any person who can read an Ordnance Survey map will have no difficulty in interpreting any chart provided that he has also a copy of chart No. 5011 which lists and explains the symbols and abbreviations used. On a chart only those features and structures that are of interest to the sailor are printed on any area that represents land, whereas the areas that represent water are covered in great detail.

British charts, printed by the Admiralty's Hydrographic Office, are in a transitional stage owing to metrication. Fathom charts giving heights in feet and depths in fathoms (6 ft) and feet have largely been replaced by metric charts. Alterations to charts and other Admiralty publications such as the *List of Lights* are given in *Notices to Mariners* which are published weekly and summarised periodically.

Charts of different scale are required for various purposes. Small-scale charts cover vast areas of ocean, medium-scale charts provide more detail about a smaller area, say a 50-mile stretch of coastline, and large-scale charts show a small area, such as a port, in great detail.

The position of a vessel or place is found by referring to the borders of the chart. The top and bottom borders show degrees, minutes and sub-divisions of minutes of longitude, while the two side borders show those of latitude. Some meridians and some parallels of latitude are printed on the chart. The latitude scale on the side border is very important because one minute of latitude equals one nautical mile, 1852 metres or 6076 feet, and all distances at sea are measured in nautical miles. The distance between any two places marked on the medium or large-scale charts normally carried on board can be measured with dividers against the latitude scale, but the top and bottom borders are never used because one minute of longitude does not represent one nautical mile. Speed at sea is based on the nautical mile and is given in knots: one knot equals one nautical mile per hour.

Numbers are printed all over the area of the chart that represents water, and each is a sounding giving the depth of water at that particular place. Lines (depth contours) connect places where the depths of water are the same. Soundings are given in fathoms and feet, or in metres below chart datum (see Fig 22) which is Lowest

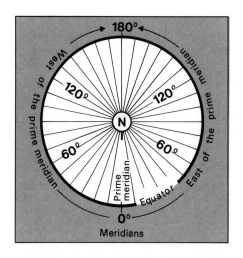

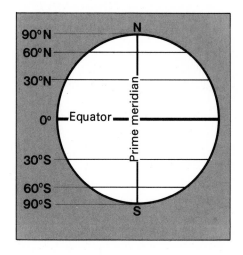

FIGURE 58: LATITUDE AND LONGITUDE

The position of a place on earth is fixed by its latitude and longitude. The prime meridian, longitude 0°, runs from the north pole, through the Greenwich Observatory in London to the south pole. Meridians run east and west from the prime meridian to the oppositie side of the earth, longitude 180°. Each degree is divided into 60 minutes and each minute into 60 seconds.

The parallels of latitude run at right angles to the meridians. The equator, latitude 0°, is midway between the poles which are latitude 90° N and S, and the parallels of latitude between the poles and the equator are similarly given in degrees minutes and seconds. A position is given as, eg, 33° 14' 25" N, 120° 38' 43" E.

WELCOME ON BOARD

Astronomical Tide on metric charts but Mean Low Water Springs on fathom charts. The title of the chart gives details of chart datum together with the measurements used, natural scale etc.

In British waters tidal range is often considerable, and a danger such as a rock may be visible at low water. A rock that covers and uncovers is marked by a special symbol, and like other features such as a sand bank that dries, is marked by an underlined figure which indicates its drying height – the height of the feature above chart datum. Heights on land and of features that do not cover at high water are given in feet or metres above Mean High Water Springs,

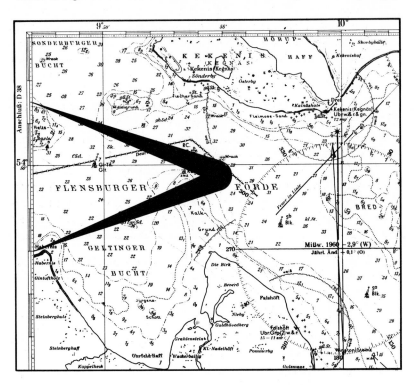

FIGURE 59: MEASURE DISTANCE AGAINST THE SIDE BORDERS

On this German chart, which is very similar to a British chart, the degrees, minutes and tenths of minutes of longitude are shown along the top border, and those of latitude along the side border. The navigator frequently needs to know a distance, say from X to Y. He spreads the dividers with one point on X and the other on Y and at about the same latitude as X and Y, he measures the distance between the points against the scale of latitude on the side border. One minute of latitude equals one nautical mile and here the distance is 3·5 minutes or 3·5 nautical miles.

86

and MHWS is also the reference level for vertical clearance of bridges and overhead cables.

Many other details are printed on charts such as the type of coast; dangers and the aids to navigation that mark them; information about tidal streams in the area; anchorages; prohibited areas and the positions of radio beacons which assist the navigator if he has radio direction-finding equipment on board.

Aids to navigation

The chart not only shows where water is shallow but also where there are dangers; for example at the mouth of a river or at a harbour entrance there is often a relatively narrow deep-water channel with sand or mud banks stretching out either side, and there may be a submerged rock in mid-channel that has to be avoided. Such hazards are marked by navigational aids such as buoys or beacons, the positions and details of which are entered on the chart.

Formerly different countries used many different buoyage systems but in European and some other waters, these are being replaced by the International Association of Lighthouse Authorities system, IALA A, which has been laid in most British waters.

Channels, estuaries and rivers are marked by the IALA A lateral system. When entering a harbour or when sailing with the main flood stream, spar buoys or flat-topped can buoys, painted red, are left to port; spar buoys or pointed-topped conical buoys, painted green, are left to starboard. At night a boat entering sees red lights to

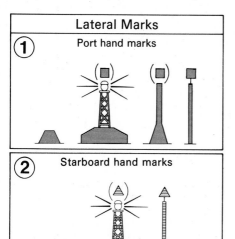

Lateral Marks

① Port hand marks

② Starboard hand marks

FIGURE 60: IALA A BUOYAGE SYSTEM – LATERAL MARKS

1. Port hand mark, red. If a topmark is carried, red can. Lights red. Leave to port when entering a harbour or when sailing with the main flood stream.

2. Starboard hand mark, green. If a topmark is carried, green cone point up. Lights green. Leave to starboard when entering a harbour or when sailing with the main flood stream.

port, exhibited by the red port hand marks, and green lights to starboard – just like her own side lights. On leaving harbour and when sailing with the ebb stream, she leaves red port hand marks to starboard and green starboard hand marks to port.

This lateral system is combined with a cardinal system based on the points of the compass. The marks are pillar or spar buoys, painted with black and yellow horizontal stripes, and they always carry two large black cone topmarks, one above the other. The name of the cardinal mark tells the navigator which side of the mark to sail to find safe water: if a danger such as a wreck is marked with a south cardinal mark, he sails to south of the mark; in a channel a west cardinal mark may be laid to show where the channel bends or divides, and he sails to the west of this mark. In the north quadrant cones both point up, and in the south quadrant both point downwards – easy to remember because north is at the top of a chart and south at the bottom. West quadrant cones are points together – turn them sideways through 90° and they look like the letter W: east quadrant cones are bases together. The lights exhibited by cardinal marks are white and either Quick Flashing (Q) at a rate of about 60 flashes each minute or Very Quick Flashing (VQ) at about double that rate. The north cardinal mark flashes continously, VQ or Q, but the others repeat a pattern over a period of 5, 10 or 15 seconds. The east cardinal mark flashes three times, either VQ(3) followed by darkness every five seconds, or Q(3) followed by darkness every ten seconds. The south cardinal mark exhibits VQ(6) plus a long flash lasting at least 2 seconds every 10 seconds or Q(6) + L.Fl·15s. The west cardinal mark's characteristic is VQ(9)10s or Q(9)15s. Isolated dangers are marked by a pillar or spar buoy laid immediately above the danger, and a boat can sail safely all round the mark. The buoy is painted with black and red horizontal bands, carries a topmark of two large black spheres one above the other, and exhibits a white light, GP.Fl(2), that is, two flashes grouped together followed by darkness.

Safe water marks are laid where there is navigable water all round, often to mark the centre of a fairway: they are spherical, spar or pillar buoys painted red and white vertically, and may exhibit a light which is either isophase (*iso*: equal intervals of light and darkness), occulting (*oc*: light lasts longer than darkness) or one long flash every ten seconds. Special marks are yellow, vary in shape, may exhibit yellow lights and/or carry topmarks shaped like a St. Andrew's cross. They mark the positions of cables, pipe lines, or special features.

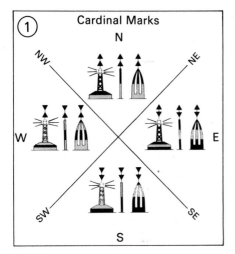

① Cardinal Marks

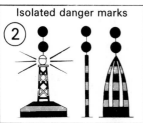

② Isolated danger marks

③ Safe water marks

FIGURE 61: – IALA A BUOYAGE – CARDINAL MARKS

1. Painted with black and yellow horizontal bands, they always carry two conical topmarks to show where safe water is found, ie to the north of a north cardinal mark, to the east of an east cardinal mark etc. The danger lies on the opposite side, ie to the north of a south cardinal mark.

2. Isolated danger: red and black horizontal bands. Topmarks, two black spheres. Laid immediately above a danger such as a single rock: safe water all round.

3. Safe water: red and white vertical stripes. If a topmark is carried, red sphere.

Other aids to navigation include manned light vessels; Lanbys (Large Automatic Navigation BuoY); beacons which are erected on shore or in shallow water, and perches which are poles rammed into the mud on either side of a small channel navigable by smaller craft. Lighthouses, built on coasts, islands and rocky ledges, exhibit direction lights which not only indicate the position of the lighthouse and of any danger that it marks but also guide a vessel clear of the danger. The structure is fixed and the light exhibited can therefore be varied from one sector to another. Frequently, the light is obscured over the sector facing towards the land and shines white over the sector in which a boat can sail safely, but the sector marking a danger may be coloured. For example, some lighthouses and direction lights exhibit red, white and green lights so that a boat approaching a harbour from seaward is in safe water when she sees the white light, is too far to port when she sees the red light and too far to starboard when the light is green.

Leading lines also assist vessels to enter and leave harbours and rivers, and their true bearings from seaward are marked on charts. If there is a single mark on shore the boat keeps the bearing on it steady. Often there are two marks on land, and they may carry lights. The boat is on the leading line when the two marks are in line; if she sails to one side of the leading line, say to starboard, the marks open and the upper mark appears to move to the right of the lower one.

Most of the light characteristics have been explained in the description of buoyage, but there are others. Fixed lights (F) are exhibited by aids on shore such as leading marks. A fixed and flashing (F.Fl) light shows a continuous light with a brighter flash at intervals. As an example of a group flashing light, the abbreviation Fl(3)10s indicates that three flashes are followed by darkness, the pattern being repeated every 10 seconds. Similary Oc(3)20s indicates a group occulting light; during every 20 second period the light eclipses three times in a group, followed by light. An alternating light (Alt) is seen to change colour when viewed from a boat making no way over the ground.

Many aids to navigation make audible signals to indicate their position in fog. These may be made only in restricted visibility, such as the sirens and foghorns sounded by lighthouses and light vessels, or, as with bell and whistle buoys, may be sounded whether visibility is good or poor when the buoy moves in response to the waves.

Navigation instruments

The Compass   The most important of the instruments that help a sailor to find his way over water is the compass, which shows direction, both the direction in which he is heading – his course –

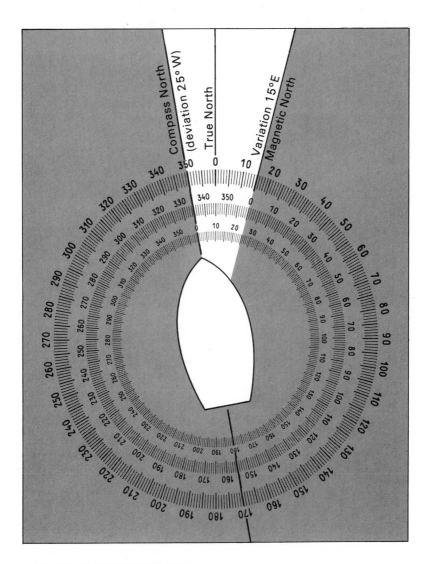

FIGURE 62: THE THREE NORTHS

The outer rose is based on true north, the geographic north pole. The middle rose is based on magnetic north, easterly variation shown here being 15°. The inside rose shows the direction indicated by the steering compass which, here, is subject to 25° of westerly deviation. Deviation is exaggerated for the sake of clarity in the drawing, and would be reduced by a compass adjuster if it were so great.

and the direction of objects outside the boat – their bearings. The magnetic steering compass used on board a sailing boat has a compass card which is marked in degrees from 0–360° and sometimes also with the 32 points of the compass. The cardinal points are north, east, south and west and there are seven points between each e.g. E, E × S, ESE, SE × E, SE, SE × S, SSE, S × E, S. × signifies 'by', thus east by south is E × S. The compass bowl is filled with liquid to damp down the movement of the card which swings round to point continuously towards north. If the course to be steered is 254° the helmsman keeps the 254° graduation mark on the compass card in line with the lubber line. This is frequently a small rod fixed to the bowl just ahead of the card, but a modern spherical compass mounted on a bulkhead may have a lubber line marked on the transparent bowl on the after side of the card.

Although the helmsman may be steering north, 000°, according to the compass card, the boat will not be heading straight towards the north pole because a magnetic compass installed in a boat is subject to two errors called variation and deviation (Fig 62).

The meridians printed on a chart point towards true north, the north pole, but a magnetic compass, such as a hand-bearing compass held well away from all disturbing influences, will point towards magnetic north which is in Canada, some 1000 miles away from the geographic north pole. Variation is the difference between the direction of magnetic north and true north; it differs from place to place and, because the magnetic north pole itself moves, it also changes annually. If the compass points further east than true north, variation, measured in degrees and minutes, is said to be easterly, but in British waters it is westerly. The exact details of variation in a specific area are printed beside the compass rose on the chart.

Deviation is caused by iron and steel objects on board, or by electric circuits and electronic apparatus installed near a magnetic compass. When a compass is fitted permanently in a boat, deviation, measured in degrees, differs according to the course steered because, when the boat alters course, the position of the disturbing influences changes in relation to the compass needles beneath the card which continue to point to compass north. The amount to allow for deviation on any particular course is found by swinging the boat through 360°, taking note of the amount of easterly or westerly error every 20° against a known bearing; then a deviation table can be drawn up and referred to at any time.

The compass course that has been steered by a boat has to be converted to a magnetic or true course before it can be entered on a chart. Assuming the compass course to be 190°, variation to be 4°W and deviation to be 2°E, the calculation is as follows:

Compass course	190°
Add easterly deviation	2°
Magnetic course	192°
Subtract westerly variation	4°
True course	188°

Conversely, if the true course has to be converted to the compass course which will be steered by the helmsman:

True course	188°
Add westerly variation	4°
Magnetic course	192°
Subtract easterly deviation	2°
Compass course	190°

One way of remembering when to add and when to subtract is to use the mnemonic CADET which starts with C for Compass and ends with T for True; the three middle letters tell you to ADd Easterly: that is, when converting from compass to true, add easterly variation and deviation, but subtract westerly variation and deviation. As in the example above, the reverse applies when working from true to compass; easterly variation and deviation are subtracted; westerly variation and deviation are added.

Bearings are converted in the same way. Suppose that the bearing of an object, 358°, is found by steering directly towards it, and that deviation is 3° east and variation 6° west:

Compass bearing	358°
Add easterly deviation	3°
Magnetic bearing	001°
Subtract westerly variation	6°
True bearing	355°

The Log The navigator also needs to know how far he has sailed through the water. This can be measured with a patent log which has a rotator streamed at the end of a long line. As the boat advances the rotator turns and drives a register which indicates the distance sailed through the water and, often, speed in knots. Boat speed can also be found by multiplying distance sailed in nautical miles by 60

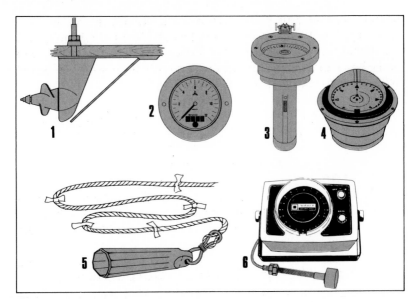

FIGURE 63: NAVIGATIONAL INSTRUMENTS

1. Sumlog. The impeller, installed beneath the hull, rotates as the boat moves through the water, the rate of rotation being transmitted mechanically or electronically to 2. a dial in the cockpit. Most logs record both speed and distance sailed through the water.

3. Traditional type hand-bearing compass with a prism and a battery in the handle for night work. Modern alternatives are much smaller.

4. Steering compass. If the bottom of the compass bowl is flat the compass has to be hung in gimbals; it will then stay level and be able to swing freely regardless of the boat's motion. With a spherical compass the card can tilt at any angle and the compass bowl need not be gimballed externally.

5. Lead and line. A heavy lump of lead is attached to a line marked at intervals to indicate depth of water. The hollow in the bottom can be filled with grease (arming the lead) to bring up a sample of the bottom so that the skipper can see whether he is anchoring on good holding ground.

6. Echo sounder with transducer which is mounted either with its face in contact with the hull, or through the hull and flush with the bottom. The transducer transmits ultrasonic signals and receives them when they are echoed back from the bottom.

and dividing the result by the time taken in minutes: e.g. if a boat sails 7nm in 1 hour 50 mins, her speed is $420 \div 110 = 3 \cdot 8$ knots. There are many alternative types of log or speedometer available today; some have an impeller which is turned by the water streaming past the hull, others are electro-magnetic and some make use of the Doppler effect.

Almost all logs suffer from one major disadvantage, they do not operate accurately or fail to record when the boat is making little headway, and the most long-established of all logs, the Dutchman's log, then comes into its own. A floating object is thrown overboard at the bows and the time the boat takes to pass the object is measured with a stopwatch at the stern. The formula is:

$$\frac{\text{Boat's length in metres} \times 2}{\text{Time in seconds}} \qquad \text{OR} \qquad \frac{\text{Boat's length in feet} \times \cdot 6}{\text{Time in seconds}}$$

$$= \text{speed in knots}$$

For example if a boat 19 ft 8 in, 6 m, long takes 6 seconds to pass a piece of cardboard thrown overboard at the bows, she is sailing at 2 knots. The rate of a tidal stream can be measured by this method when the boat is at anchor.

Lead and echo sounder Depth of water can be measured with a lump of lead attached to a line which is marked either every metre or in feet and fathoms, but larger boats often carry an echo sounder. This measures the time that it takes for sound to travel to the bottom of the sea and back to the boat, and the time is indicated on a dial marked in fathoms or metres. As well as warning the helmsman when the boat is sailing into shallow water, an echo sounder can help the navigator to fix his position; in waters where depths alter quickly he can compare the soundings recorded with the soundings marked on the chart.

Plotting instruments As well as dividers to measure distances, the navigator needs a soft pencil, a rubber and a plotting instrument. When he works out the course to steer he draws a line on the chart

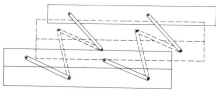

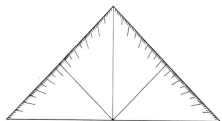

FIGURE 64: NAVIGATIONAL INSTRUMENTS: PARALLEL RULER AND PROTRACTOR

from the boat's position to his objective and needs to know the angle that this line makes with north. If he uses parallel rulers, the traditional plotting instrument, he lines them up on the course and, taking care not to let them slip, opens and closes them alternately, moving them over to the nearest compass rose where he reads off the true course against the true rose or the magnetic course against the magnetic rose which is usually printed inside the true rose (Fig 64). Alternatively he may use a triangular protractor graduated in degrees from a centre midway along the hypotenuse. He lines the hypotenuse up with the course, slides the protractor along a ruler or another protractor until the centre point is exactly on a meridian and reads the true course at the point where the meridian cuts the graduation on the protractor.

Similarly, if he has taken a magnetic bearing of an object on land with the hand-bearing compass, he can line up the parallel ruler with the bearing on the magnetic rose and 'walk' the rulers over to the symbol on the chart that marks the object's position, drawing the line of bearing to seaward of the symbol. Alternatively he first converts the magnetic bearing to a true bearing, then places the protractor with the centre of the hypotenuse and the graduation matching the true bearing both on one meridian, and slides the protractor along a ruler to the chart symbol. There are many other instruments of this kind, such as patented protractors and rulers, and each navigator has his favourite.

Coastal navigation

First the navigator has to work out the safe course to steer. In non-tidal waters he simply draws a line on the chart between his position and the point he is aiming for, checking that this does not lead him near any dangers, converts the true course on the chart to a compass course (page 93), allows for leeway if necessary, and tells the helmsman what course to steer. Leeway is greatest when the boat is close-hauled, unimportant when broad reaching and nil when running, but varies not only from boat to boat but with conditions. Leeway can be estimated from the angle the boat's fore-and-aft line makes with the line of the turbulent water of her wake streaming astern.

In tidal waters the effect of the tidal stream also has to be allowed for, as in Figure 65, and the approximate rate and set during the hour(s) the boat will be sailing on any particular course can be found from the tide tables and tidal stream atlas.

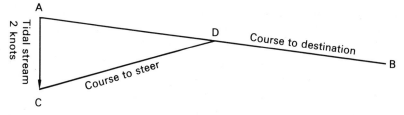

FIGURE 65: ALLOWING FOR THE TIDAL STREAM

The navigator draws the course he wishes to make good, line AB. In a flat calm a boat at A, not using her engines, would drift with the tidal stream, and the line AC shows the direction (set) and the distance she would be carried based on the rate at which the stream runs, say 2 knots. A boat making way under sail in any direction from A is also set in this direction by the tidal stream and AC, 2 nautical miles in length, indicates how far she will be carried in one hour. During the same hour the boat is expected to broad reach at 5 knots and, a line, 5 nm in length, is drawn from C, cutting AB at D. CD is the course to steer. Although the boat will be making good course ADB over the ground her fore-and-aft line will be parallel to CD, the course she will make good through the water.

During the period that the boat is sailing along this course the navigator checks her position from time to time. If in sight of land he generally takes bearings of objects that he can identify as marked on the chart. When using a hand-bearing compass both hands are needed to hold it steady and level, and he braces himself firmly, well clear of the standing rigging, pulpit and guardrail so that the compass is not deflected by them. The prism or sights are aligned with the object, and the bearing is read on the compass card. When the bearing is plotted on the chart a position line is obtained, and the boat must be somewhere on this line. A second bearing, taken on a different object, provides a second position line and, provided that the bearings have been taken accurately and that there is no deviation, the boat must be at the point where the two lines cross. (See Fig 66). A magnetic bearing has to be converted to a true bearing if it is referred to a meridian which points to true north, but can be laid off without being converted if it is referred to the magnetic rose.

The steering compass can also be used, say if the boat has no hand-bearing compass. Sometimes it is so mounted that the object can be sighted directly over the compass, but often the helmsman alters course and, when he is heading straight for the object, the boat's course matches the bearing of the object. This is a compass bearing and has to be corrected to a magnetic or true bearing before it can be laid off on the chart.

Position lines can be obtained in many other ways, but the simplest and most reliable is a transit. When two objects marked on the chart are identified and are seen to come into line the boat must be somewhere on the extension seaward of the line between the two objects, and there can be no error because no instruments are used.

The boat may be out of sight of land, landmarks may be few and far between or difficult to identify, and the boat's position then can only be estimated. Suppose that her position was fixed at 1100 hrs, log reading 5 n.m. and that an hour later the log reads 9 n.m. The navigator finds the boat's dead reckoning (DR) position by drawing a line from the fix to represent the course steered by the helmsman during those 60 minutes, allowing for leeway if necessary. The length of the line is 4 n.m., the distance she has sailed through the water. In tidal waters the navigator draws a line from the DR position to represent the effect of the tidal stream; the direction of the line shows the set between 1100 and 1200 hrs, while its length represents the rate of, say, 2 knots during the same period. The boat's estimated position is 2 n.m. from her DR position, and the

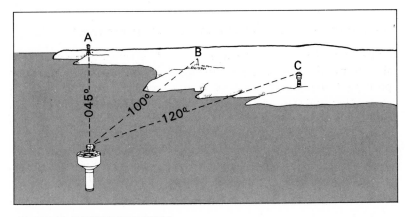

FIGURE 66: TAKING BEARINGS

The navigator selects at least two landmarks, the positions of which are marked on the chart. When two bearings are plotted on the chart they should meet as nearly at a right angle as possible to provide a reliable fix; he therefore avoids landmarks that are too close to each other because the angle would be too acute, or too far apart – angle too obtuse. A landmark close to the boat is preferable to one further away because the motion of a small boat may cause errors when taking bearings with a hand-bearing compass, and the more distant the object the greater the error. Three identified landmarks provides a more reliable fix; the three bearings are taken in quick succession and, when plotted, the position lines frequently form a small triangle known as a cocked hat. The boat's position is taken to be somewhere within the cocked hat.

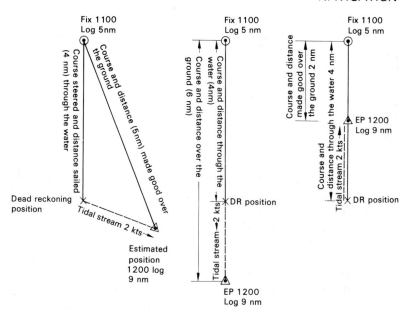

FIGURE 66A: DEAD RECKONING AND ESTIMATED POSITIONS

course and distance she has actually made good over the ground is shown by the line between the original fix and her estimated position. If the tidal stream was fair and setting in the same direction as the boat's course she will have made good 6 n.m. over the ground, but if the tidal stream was foul she will only have made good 2 n.m. during the hour.

The boat's position can only be worked up this way if the time of every alteration of course is noted in the log-book, together with the distance logged at that moment. Alterations in wind strength and direction, and any other factors which affect the boat's speed, are also noted.

A position found in this way cannot be relied upon because the effect of tidal streams and leeway has to be estimated and because the helmsman cannot state exactly what course he has steered; it is therefore essential to fix the boat's position by taking bearings whenever an opportunity occurs. Many boats now carry radio direction-finding instruments with which the navigator obtains bearings on radio beacons sited close by the coast or in lightvessels. These are particularly helpful in restricted visibility and when out of sight of land, and if the beacon is not too far distant are laid off on the chart in the same way as visual bearings.

99

Navigation at night can be confusing for a novice when he sees lights of various colours all around, and he should be safely in harbour before night falls, but an experienced navigator can fix his position as easily by night as by day, and when visibility is poor it is often easier to identify a light just before dawn than the lighthouse when the sun has risen. Coastal navigation is largely a question of

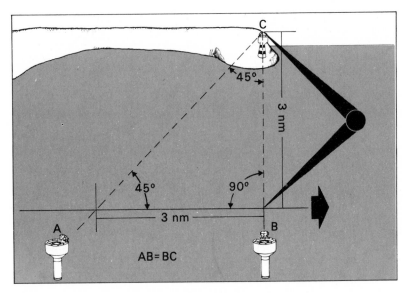

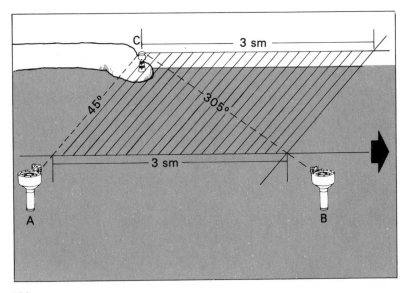

taking care, using common sense and gaining experience. Celestial navigation, used when far out of sight of land, requires additional instruments and reference books, and is an entirely separate art.

FIGURE 67: FOUR POINT BEARING AND DOUBLING THE ANGLE ON THE BOW

Each of the 32 points of the compass equals $11^1/_4$°, and four points equals 45°. The navigator takes two relative bearings (bearings referred to the fore-and-aft line, dead ahead being 0° and dead astern 180°) on some object on shore, C, which need not be marked on the chart. The first relative bearing is taken at A, 45°, and the second at B, 90° when the object is abeam. ABC is a right-angled triangle and AB = AC. By calculating the distance the boat has sailed over the ground from A to B the navigator establishes distance off, BC, which is 3 n.m. in the figure. In non-tidal waters and at slack water the distance sailed by the boat through the water, as measured by the log, is the same as the distance sailed over the ground, but if the tidal stream is fair the distance that she has been set during the period that elapses between taking bearings, say 1 n.m., has to be added to the distance sailed through the water and she will have covered 4 n.m. over the ground: BC then will be 4 n.m. If the tidal stream is foul the distance is subtracted from the distance logged and she will only be 2 n.m. from the lighthouse.

The same principle applies in the case of doubling the angle on the bow. The first relative bearing is taken, say, when the object bears 30°, the second when it bears 60°, and the distance made good over the ground during this period is calculated. Because ABC is an isosceles triangle AB again equals AC. By producing the course line AB the navigator can see in advance whether his course will lead him clear of, say, a headland with off-lying rocks.

FIGURE 68: RUNNING FIX

If there is only one identifiable object in sight the navigator first takes a bearing at A, 045° in the figure; then he sails a steady course for a certain period and takes a second bearing, in this case 305° and checks the log to find how far the boat has sailed through the water during this period. He lays off the first bearing on the chart and, from any point A on this position line he draws a line AB which represents the course and distance sailed over the ground, (ie course and distance through the water plus allowance for the set and rate of the tidal stream) and then transfers the position line along AB, drawing it parallel to AC through point B. He enters the second bearing and the boat's position is at D, where the second position line cuts the transferred position line.

Lights, flags and signals

Lights and shapes

A vessel exhibits navigation lights when under way at night, both to draw attention to herself and to enable other vessels to know in which direction she is sailing. The *International Collision Regulations for Preventing Collisions at Sea* stipulate which lights are to be exhibited and where, the sectors over which they must shine, and their intensity. They also prescribe the lights and shapes that must be exhibited by various classes of vessels that manoeuvre with difficulty, and by those that are anchored or aground. Lights are exhibited from sunset to sunrise, and during the day when visibility is restricted, say by snow or heavy rain. Shapes are hoisted aloft by day.

The side lights, green to starboard and red to port, shine over a sector of 112·5° from dead ahead to two points abaft the beam; the white stern light shines over an arc of 135°, 67·5° either side of dead astern; the white masthead light shines over the sectors covered by both side lights, 225°; all-round lights may be red, green or white and shine through 360°.

A sailing vessel under way exhibits only side lights and stern light, but side lights fixed in their normal position by the coachroof are often masked by the genoa. She may instead carry a bi-colour lantern at the bow, showing both port and starboard side lights, or a tri-colour lantern at or near the masthead, exhibiting the stern light as well as both side lights. A third alternative is to carry normal side and stern lights near the deck plus two all round lights near the top of the mast, the upper being red and the lower green.

A sailing boat using her engine ranks as power-driven, whether her sails are hoisted or not, and she therefore exhibits a masthead light in addition to side and stern lights. She should carry a cone forward by day, point down. Power-driven vessels over 164 ft (50 m) in length must carry a second and higher masthead light further aft, and many smaller power-driven vessels do so as well. Small boats under 23 ft (7 m) in length are only obliged to carry a torch or white lantern, but obviously it is sensible and safer to show the side and stern lights prescribed for larger boats, and the masthead light if under engine. An all round white light, the riding light, indicates that a boat is at anchor.

On the water a vessel that is overtaking another will at first see only the white stern light of the boat ahead but, as she overtakes, say to starboard, the white light is obscured and is replaced by the green side light and white masthead light of a power-driven vessel, or by the green side light of a boat under sail. The overtaken vessel, on the other hand, sees first the overtaking boat's red port light, and her masthead light if she is power-driven, but as she passes these are obscured and are replaced by the white stern light.

When a sailing boat under engine is on a reciprocal course with a large power-driven vessel, the two boats approach each other head-on; the sailing boat sees the other's red and green side lights simultaneously and the masthead lights will be in line. When both vessels comply with the Regulations by altering course to starboard the green starboard light is obscured and the two masthead lights separate. The vessels pass port side to port side, red to red.

If a helmsman sees cones, cylinders or balls hoisted in rigging by day, or an unusual combination of lights being exhibited either in addition to the normal navigation lights carried by a boat under way, or in addition to a riding light, he should keep well clear until the skipper has checked their meaning in the *Collision Regulations* because they warn that a vessel is either not under command or is unable to manoeuvre freely, towing, fishing, etc. The *Regulations* are printed in *Reeds Nautical Almanac* and can be obtained from the Royal Yachting Association.

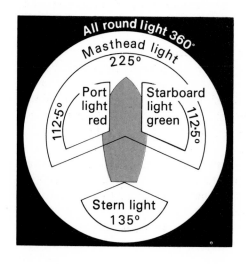

FIGURE 69: LIGHTS EXHIBITED BY VESSELS

Port light, red 112·5°: starboard light, green 112·5°: masthead light, white 225°: all round light, 360°: stern light, white 135°.

Sound signals

The *Collision Regulations* also specify what sound signals a vessel is to make when manoeuvring in sight of another to inform her as to what she is doing. A short blast lasts about 1 second and a long blast 4 to 6 seconds:

·   I am altering course to starboard
· ·   I am altering course to port
· · ·   I am operating astern propulsion
· · · · ·   either: I am doubtful about your intentions or actions
         or: I am doubtful that you are taking sufficient action to avoid collision
—   Warning signal on approaching a bend or some area where a vessel may be hidden by a building or an obstruction.

In a narrow channel or fairway:

— — ·   I intend to overtake on your starboard side
— — · ·   I intend to overtake on your port side
— · — ·   I am in agreement with your intention to overtake.

Fog signals   Sound signals are also made in fog and when visibility is poor:

—   One long blast at least every two minutes is sounded by a power-driven vessel making way
— —   Two long blasts in succession at least every two minutes are sounded by a vessel that is not at anchor, moored or aground, but is stopped and not making way through the water
— · ·   One long and two short blasts are sounded at least every two minutes by sailing vessels and by several other classes of vessel that cannot manoeuvre freely.

     A bell rung rapidly for about 5 seconds every minute gives warning of a boat at anchor. A small sailing boat with no bell makes a noise by whatever method is most effective, and the farther the sound carries the better.

Storm signals

British coastal stations hoist storm cones by day, and exhibit three red lights by night in the form of a triangle, to give visual warnings of approaching gales. The north cone is hoisted point up by day, and the lights point up by night, when a gale or storm is expected from a northerly direction. A south cone or three lights, point down, indicate that a gale is expected from a southerly direction. Boats that cruise or race along the coast or offshore boats carry a radio so that the crew can listen to shipping forecasts which give gale and storm warnings at the beginning and end of each forecast.

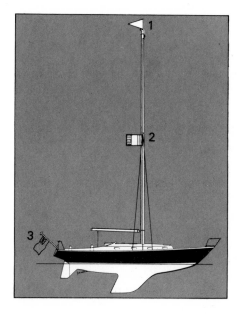

FIGURE 70: FLAGS WORN BY A SAILING BOAT

1. Club burgee. 2. Courtesy flag, a small foreign national flag worn at the starboard spreader when in harbour. 3. Ensign: may be worn at the mizzen masthead of a yawl or ketch.

Flags

Centreboard dinghies normally only wear a racing flag or club burgee at the masthead, but larger sailing boats wear an ensign in addition, to indicate their nationality. The white ensign is worn only by naval vessels and by vessels belonging to members of the Royal Yacht Squadron. Blue ensigns, sometimes defaced (with a symbol in the blue part) are worn by vessels belonging to government departments, such as HM Customs, and by vessels owned by members of certain yacht clubs. A defaced red ensign with the badge of a club in the fly, is worn by vessels owned by members of that particular club. A warrant to fly any of these ensigns is issued to the owner of a sailing boat by the Ministry of Defence, and only the burgee of the club granted the privilege of wearing a special ensign may be worn with that ensign. A red ensign may be worn by any British yacht.

The ensign is worn near the stern, and is normally hoisted on a staff right aft when entering or leaving harbour, and when at anchor or moored in harbour. When dipped as a mark of respect, say to salute a naval vessel, it is lowered about two-thirds of the way down the staff and is not rehoisted until the vessel being saluted has dipped and rehoisted her ensign in acknowledgement. Ensigns are usually lowered at sea.

The burgee, worn at the top of the mast or mainmast, indicates the club to which the owner belongs. It is hoisted when the crew go on board and lowered when they go on shore. The ensign and the burgee are hoisted at 0800 in the summer and at 0900 in the winter when the crew is on board in harbour, and they are lowered at sunset. At sea the burgee is often left hoisted at night to indicate wind direction. A flag officer of a yacht or sailing club flies a broad pennant in place of a club burgee. When racing the burgee is frequently replaced by a racing flag.

A courtesy flag is worn in harbour at the starboard spreader when visiting a foreign country, and is usually the national flag of that country. A protest flag is flown when a protest is made against another competitor during a race. Some owners fly the RYA flag from the spreader to indicate their membership of that Association.

The set of *International Code of Signals* flags consists of 26 letters, 10 numeral pendants, three substitutes and the code and answering pendant. These flags are used to send messages visually, and the important single letter signals are given in *Reeds Nautical Alamanc*, together with some two letter signals. Code flags are also used when racing, code flag P being broken out as the preparatory signal five minutes before the starting gun, and the boats themselves may be required to fly a code flag from the backstay to indicate the class in which they are sailing.

On special occasions vessels in harbour dress overall by stringing all the code flags together and hoisting them to form a continuous line from stem to masthead to stern; burgee and ensign are also worn on these occasions.

Distress signals

There are many internationally recognised distress signals listed in the *Collision Regulations*, and some have already been mentioned. The dinghy sailor who cannot right his boat raises and lowers outstretched arms to either side slowly and repeatedly. Larger keelboats carry flares or rockets that show red lights or stars, or make orange smoke. They may also hoist international code flag N over C, or a square flag over a round shape such as a ball, or may sound a foghorn continuously. The signal sent by radio telegraphy is 'Mayday', while SOS · · · − − − · · · can be made by any means

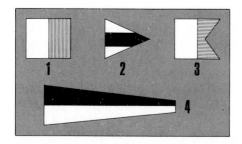

FIGURE 71: FLAG SHAPES

1. Flag 2. Burgee 3. Broad pennant 4. pennant.

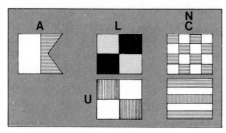

FIGURE 72: IMPORTANT INTERNATIONAL CODE FLAG SIGNALS

A white and blue: I have a diver down. Keep well clear at slow speed
L yellow and black: Stop your vessel instantly
U red and white: You are running into danger
N over C: blue and white over blue-white-red-white-blue: International distress signal.

available such as radiotelegraphy (RT), foghorn or flashing light. Large vessels may fire a gun every minute, or may set fire to an object such as a tar barrel.

Distress signals must be reserved purely for a genuine emergency when a vessel needs immediate outside assistance.

Transporting a boat on land

The simplest and cheapest method of transporting a small boat or sailboard on land is on the roof of a car, but few cars can carry a weight in excess of 130 lbs (60 kg). The roof rack must be strong enough to carry the boat, and so securely fastened to the car that it will not slip if the brakes have to be applied vigorously. No speed limit applies when carrying a car-top dinghy, but lift generated when the car travels at speed acts upwards if the boat is carried keel down in her natural floating position. It is therefore better to load a dinghy or sailboard upside down, lashed firmly to the roof rack. The load on the roof increases resistance and, consequently, petrol consumption. Driving can be unpleasant if there is a strong side wind.

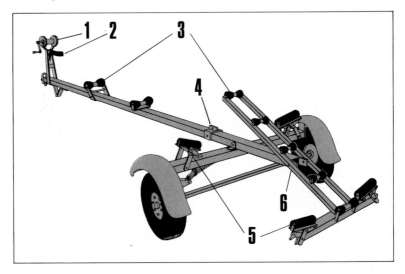

FIGURE 73 : TRAILER WITH TILT FRAME

1. Winch for launching the boat and for hauling her on to the trailer. 2. Stem fitting on the winch post. 3. Keel rollers. 4. Locking catch for the tilt frame. 5. Bilge chock rollers. 6. Tilt frame.

Heavier boats have to be transported by trailer, and there are two points to bear in mind. First, the carrying capacity of the trailer, which is specified by the manufacturer, and second, the towing capacity of the motor car, that is, the weight of the trailer with its load. Towing capacity varies from make to make, and although

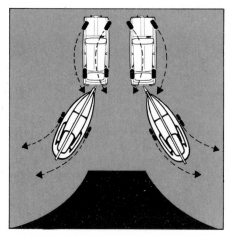

FIGURE 74: REVERSING A TRAILER

The driver has to think backwards because he has to turn the steering wheel in the opposite direction to that in which he turns it when reversing the car. If the trailer is to be turned to the left he turns the steering wheel to the right — the back of the car then turns to the right and the trailer turns to the left. And vice versa if the trailer is to be turned to the right.

trailers are obtainable that can carry boats weighing up to 4·5 tonnes, a powerful vehicle is required to tow them.

Maximum speed when towing is limited in Britain to 50 mph (80 km/hr) but speed limits vary from country to country and should be checked before going abroad, together with regulations concerning maximum permitted length, lights and signs that have to be carried if the mast projects beyond the boat, etc. The lighting board carries reflectors and brake lights, as well as the registration number of the towing vehicle. When driving with a trailer the brakes have to be applied earlier and gradually; stopping distance is greater and may be as much as double that of the car alone.

Most trailers have an adjustable axle and winch post so that the load can be correctly balanced, and often the chocks and keel rollers can also be moved to support the boat firmly. Weight should be concentrated over the axle; if it is too far back the trailer raises the car's rear wheels and contact with the road is reduced; if the boat is nose heavy the front wheels are lifted and steering is affected.

Many harbours have a launching slip where dinghies and smaller keelboats with a centreboard or retractable keel can be launched directly from the trailer. Trailers with a tilt frame and winch forward are available for larger boats. When wheels are immersed in salt water the brake drums should be flushed out with fresh water and well greased. Tyres must be kept at the pressure recommended by the manufacturer. Larger keelboats are launched by crane, but small dinghies are frequently removed from the trailer and transported to the water by a trolley.

Beaufort wind scale

Beaufort Number	Mean Wind Speed (Knots)	Descriptive Term	Deep Sea Criterion	Probable height of waves in metres
0	less than 1	Calm	Sea like a mirror.	0
1	1–3	Light air	Ripples with the appearance of scales are formed but without foam crests.	0·1
2	4–6	Light breeze	Small wavelets, still short but more pronounced. Crests have a glassy appearance and do not break.	0·2
3	7–10	Gentle breeze	Large wavelets. Crests begin to break. Foam of glassy appearance. Perhaps scattered white horses.	0·6
4	11–16	Moderate breeze	Small waves, becoming longer, fairly frequent white horses.	1·0
5	17–21	Fresh breeze	Moderate waves, taking a more pronounced form; many white horses are formed (chance of some spray).	2·0

6	22–27	Strong breeze	Large waves begin to form, the white foam crests are more extensive everywhere (probably some spray).	3·0
7	28–33	Near gale	Sea heaps up and white foam from breaking waves begins to be blown in streaks along the direction of the wind.	4·0
8	34–40	Gale	Moderately high waves of greater length; edges of crests begin to break into spindrift. The foam is blown in well-marked streaks along the direction of the wind.	5·5
9	41–47	Strong gale	High waves. Dense streaks of foam along the direction of the wind. Crests of waves begin to topple, tumble and roll over. Spray may affect visibility.	7·0
10	48–55	Storm	Very high waves with long overhanging crests. The resulting foam	9·0

			in great patches is blown in dense white streaks along the direction of the wind. On the whole the surface of the sea takes a white appearance. The tumbling of the sea becomes heavy and shocklike. Visibility affected.	
11	56–63	Violent storm	Exceptionally high waves. (Small and medium-sized ships might be for a time lost to view behind the waves). The sea is completely covered with long white patches of foam lying along the direction of the wind. Everywhere the edges of the wave crests are blown into froth. Visibility affected.	11·5
12	64 +	Hurricane	The air is filled with foam and spray. Sea completely white with driving spray. Visibility very seriously affected.	14 +

Glossary

BACK	1. Of the wind, to shift anticlockwise (e.g. from SW to S or E to NE); opp to veer. 2. To sheet a sail so that the wind acts on what is normally its lee side; the sail is then said to be aback.
BEAM	1. The breadth of a boat. 2. One of the transverse members that support the deck. 3. On the beam: at right angles to the centreline.
BEAR AWAY	To alter course away from the wind by putting the tiller to windward.
BEAT	To sail towards the wind, following a zigzag course first on one tack and then on the other (verb and noun).
BERTH	1. A place where a boat lies when in harbour; she may be at anchor, at a mooring, tied up alongside a quay or pontoon, tied fore-and-aft between piles, etc. 2. A place where one of the crew sleeps on board.
BOW	1. As opposed to stern, the forward end of the boat. 2. On the bow is a direction from the boat between ahead and on the beam.
BOWSPRIT	Spar that projects forward of the bow.
BUOYANCY	1. A boat floats because the force of buoyancy thrusting upwards opposes the downward acting force of gravity. 2. In general usage, the word buoyancy is used for anything that keeps a capsized boat afloat when full of water, such as watertight compartments, air-filled bags, foam-filled areas etc.
BURGEE	Small triangular flag worn at the masthead to indicate the direction of the wind.
CLEAT	A fitting to which ropes may be made fast; either a fitting with two horns (see Fig 19), or a cam cleat or jam cleat as in Fig 11. As a verb, to make a rope fast on a cleat.
DECK	The uppermost and almost horizontal part of the hull; covers a space beneath, such as the cabin or fo'c's'le.

DISPLACEMENT

A floating boat makes a 'hole' in the water, and a heavy boat makes a bigger hole than a light boat. The displacement of a keelboat is her weight, which is equal to the weight of the volume of the water that she displaces, that is, of the water that would fill that hole.

DRAW

1. A sail is said to draw when it is full of wind. 2. A boat is said to draw a certain amount of water; she would draw 3 ft if her draught is 3 ft, and will not float in water that is less than 3 ft deep.

EASE

To let out a sheet so that the sail sets at a greater angle to the centreline (c.f. harden).

FENDER

Resilient, cushion-like object which is hung over the side when the boat is moored alongside a pier, pontoon or boat to protect the topsides from damage.

FLOOR

Not a horizontal surface to walk on, but a vertical member fitted ₊transversely across the keel to connect the two sides of the hull. Frames may be fastened to the floors on either side.

FRAME

One of the ribs which make up part of the skeleton of a boat. Planking or plating is fastened to the frames to form the skin or shell of the hull.

FULLY-BATTENED

The battens run full length from luff to leech.

SAIL
GO ABOUT

To change from one tack to the other by putting the tiller to leeward; the boat luffs up into the wind and continues to turn until the sails fill on the new tack (c.f. gybe).

GRP – GLASS REINFORCED PLASTICS

Synthetic material of which many boats are made, whether large or small. The moulding consists of several laminates, each consisting of glassfibre reinforcing mat or cloth impregnated with resin, laid up one above the other in or over a mould.

GUNWALE

Broadly, the top of the sides of a boat.

GYBE

To change from one tack to the other by putting the tiller to windward; the boat bears away and, as the stern swings through the wind, the mainsail and boom slam over on to the opposite side (c.f. go about).

HARDEN To haul on a sheet, pulling in the sail so that it sets closer to the centreline (c.f. ease).

HEAD 1. The front end of a boat, from which heading – the direction in which she sails. 2. The upper corner of a triangular sail, the upper edge of a quadrilateral sail and the upper end of a part, e.g. masthead, stemhead.

HOIST 1. To raise an object such as a sail or spar. 2. The rope with which an object is raised.

HORSE Rod or wire, fitted athwartships, on which runs a block through which the mainsheet or the sheet of a boom jib is rove. The mainsheet horse is raised above the tiller and bolted to the deck either side.

INFLATABLE A rubber dinghy.

KEEL 1. The main backbone of a boat, whether she is a keelboat or a virtually flat-bottomed dinghy. Runs fore-and-aft along the centreline between stem and stern. 2. More widely applied to the entire area of a keelboat that extends downwards beneath the hull.

KNOT Unit of speed: one nautical mile per hour.

LAUNCH 1. To put a boat into the water. 2. A small boat with an inboard engine, used to ferry the crew to a boat moored offshore, etc.

LEE,
LEEWARD Away from the wind, as opposed to windward and weather.

LEEBOARD 1. Wooden plank, cloth or netting extending along the open side of a berth to prevent the crew from falling out when the boat heels. 2. One of two boards which pivot either side of a flat-bottomed vessel. The leeward leeboard is lowered to discourage her from making leeway (typical of traditional Dutch boats).

LEEWARD See Lee above.

LEEWAY See Way below.

LIST To lean to one side, not temporarily as a result of wind pressure (heeling) but permanently, generally owing to there being more weight on that side of the boat than the other.

LUFF 1. The leading edge of a sail, usually hanked to a stay (jib and genoa) or attached to a mast (mainsail and mizzen). 2. To luff up is to alter course towards the wind by putting the tiller to leeward (c.f. bear away).

MAKE 1. Make fast or belay is to attach a rope to a cleat, ring, fitting etc. 2. A boat makes way when moving through the water (see Way below), and makes 2 knots when moving at a rate of 2 nautical miles per hour.

MEMBER A part of the skeleton of the hull, such as a wooden frame or the stem, or a stringer laminated into a GRP hull to increase fore-and-aft strength.

MITRE The seam of a sail (usually a headsail) that runs from clew to luff. The cloths above the mitre run at right angles to the leech; those below run at right angles to the foot.

MOTION The movement of a boat as she responds to seas. She pitches when she see-saws back and forth longitudinally, she rolls from side to side and she yaws when she swings to either side of her course.

PIPE COT Sleeping berth made of canvas stretched inside a tubular framework.

PITCH See motion above, and p. 28 (propeller pitch).

POINT Verb relating to the course of a close-hauled boat in relation to the wind direction. She is said to point well when sailing close to the wind, to outpoint another boat when sailing higher or closer to the wind, etc. 2. Point of the compass: one of the 32 points into which the compass card is divided, $11^1/_4°$.

PORT When looking towards the bow, the equivalent of left (opp. starboard).

PRAM Small sailing dinghy with a transom at the bow as well as at the stern.

QUARTER The side of the boat between the stern and amidships, hence quartering wind and seas which blow from and approach from a direction between astern and abeam.

RAKE	The fore-and-aft angle that is made with the vertical by a part of the boat, such as the mast or the counter.
REEVE	To feed a rope through an opening, such as through a block or eye, or over a sheave. Past tense rove, opp. unreeve.
RESERVE BUOYANCY	Additional buoyancy provided by the watertight parts of the hull which are above the water when the boat is floating on her normal waterline.
ROOT BERTH	A canvas berth; the canvas is extended by a pole which is supported in sockets at either end.
ROVE	See Reeve.
RUBBING STRAKE	An additional strake or thickening of a GRP moulding provided just beneath deck level to protect the topsides from damage.
SAIL TIERS	Strips of canvas or short lengths of shock cord with which a sail may be secured to the boom etc when it has been lowered.
SCOW	A small beamy dinghy, often with a lugsail; generally designed for single-handed sailing.
SCULL	To propel a dinghy with one oar by working it back and forth in a figure of eight pattern over the stern.
SEA	1. An area of water. 2. A single wave.
SHEAVE	A small wheel over which a rope runs; may be part of a block or fitted in a spar, e.g. at the masthead for the mainsail halyard.
SHIP	1. A large vessel. 2. To place an object in its working position, such as the rudder of a sailing dinghy, or an outboard engine (opp. unship). 3. To take on board, such as a sea that breaks into the cockpit.
SIT OUT	To use crew weight to keep the boat upright and on an even keel by sitting on the gunwale and leaning back to windward so as to counter the pressure of the wind on the sails.
SOUND	1. To measure the depth of water. 2. To make a sound signal.
STARBOARD	When looking towards the bow, the equivalent of right (opp. port).
STEM	The foremost member of the skeleton of a boat; extends upwards from the keel. The planking or

plating of the sides of the hull is fastened to the stem.

STEP   1. To place a mast in its proper position; the stays and shrouds are then set up to hold it in place.   2. The fitting to which the foot of the mast is secured or the aperture in which the foot is stepped.

STRINGER   Stiffening member that runs longitudinally along the sides of the boat; is fastened to the frames of a wooden or metal hull.

TACK   1. A boat is said to be on a tack, except when she is in the process of gybing or going about; she is on starboard tack when the wind is blowing on her starboard side and she is carrying her mainboom to port, or on port tack when the wind is on her port side and her mainboom is to starboard.   2. As a verb, to change tacks, synonymous with going about (see above).   3. The forward lower corner of a sail; of jib and genoa the corner nearest the stem, of mainsail and mizzen the corner close by the gooseneck.

TRIM   1. Of sails, to alter their position in relation to the centreline by hardening or easing the sheets.   2. To move weight on board to adjust the fore-and-aft angle at which the boat floats. If a boat is trimmed by the stern her bows are higher and her stern more deeply immersed than normal.

VEER   1. Of wind, to shift clockwise (e.g. from S to SW, or NE to E).   2. To let out more anchor cable.

WAY   A boat makes way when she moves through the water, is under way when she is not moored, anchored or aground, gathers way when her speed increases, loses way when she slows and comes to a halt, and carries her way when she continues to move through the water purely on account of her momentum. She makes headway when moving forward, sternway when moving stern first and leeway when she sags to leeward of her course.

WEATHER   See Windward.

WINDWARD   Towards the wind, as opposed to leeward and lee.

Index